The Working Workbook

The Working Workbook

◆

Earning a Buck and Keeping It Coming

Camille Leon

iUniverse, Inc.
New York Lincoln Shanghai

The Working Workbook
Earning a Buck and Keeping It Coming

iUniverse, Inc.

For information address:
iUniverse, Inc.
2021 Pine Lake Road, Suite 100
Lincoln, NE 68512
www.iuniverse.com

ISBN: 0-595-27116-2

Printed in the United States of America

Contents

CHAPTER 1   Right Now! 1

CHAPTER 2   Know Yourself. 8

CHAPTER 3   Know The Employer 16

CHAPTER 4   Know Your Competition. 28

CHAPTER 5   Show That You Know What You Know 29

CHAPTER 6   Show What You Know 97

About the Author 101

Acknowledgments

I've spent several years putting this together and have many friends and associates that I want to thank. Let me take this opportunity to do so.

For their personal presence and for giving an honest (you were honest, weren't you?) appraisal of this work before it was published: John Anderson, Andres Orozco, Gerrit Kruidhof, Allen Rubinstein, Regent St. Claire, and Phillip Frazier. I'd also like to thank Jonathan Pink, for surprising me with his wonderful help, and Patricia Fripp, a motivational author and speaker, who had a greater impact on me than either of us realized…

For their work with the Orange County Employment Action Network, and it's many partner agencies, which started the ball rolling: Karen Rewers, Sarah Sheldon, Christine Couturie, Patti Long, Colleen Hodge, Larry Haynes, Sister Kathy Stein, Marie Rainwater, Anne Halapua, Cindy Campbell, and Frances Cadenas.

For their work at The WorkPlace and for keeping the ball rolling: Dora Magdaleno, James McDugle, Vishal Sharma, Joyce Roessler, Armando Lojero, Pedro Solis, and Lupe Barron.

Most importantly, Bernie Weeks, John Janda, Dianne Russell, and Charlene Ashendorf have mentored me, encouraged me, and put up with me through thick and thin!

Of course, I have to thank my mother, my grandmother, my aunt and uncle-in-law, and my uncle and aunt-in-law for always believing in me!

This list would not be complete if I didn't also thank my many Friends from Orange County and Santa Monica Friends' Meetings. Thank you all for holding me in the Light!

1

Right Now!

I can change my clothes,
I can change my mind,
I can change my attitude!
RIGHT NOW!

Right now, I can change my life!

You have secrets and understandings within you that you don't even know you possess. After all, you're old enough to have had experiences, to have learned some truths, to have seen others trying to get a job and keep it. Very likely, though, you've also learned some 'popular culture' guidelines about getting and keeping work as well as the words and admonishments of others in your life (your mother, your father, your husband (or your ex-husband), your brothers and sisters, your friends). This workbook is meant to help you sort out what is true for you and best for you. What works best for *you,* not what works best for other people. Of course, sometimes what works best for others will work best for you; still, it's important to sort through the clutter and find yourself.

This book also offers many 'tips' for 'turning over a new leaf' or 'making a fresh start.' You are welcome to take these tips with a grain of salt. Your past has already been lived, but your future is a blank slate. Your future is now open to new challenges, new opportunities, new possibilities. You probably want to fill your future with more money, more respect, more opportunities, more choices, and more time for yourself and your family. In order to turn your life around, you will probably need more money. This, in turn, will lead to more time, more respect, more choices and more opportunities. Therefore, let's focus on the best, fastest way to get more money—getting a job (and keeping it)!

Remember—It is not where you have been, it is where you want to go and what you are willing to change to get there.

This book is for those starting out for the first time or starting out for the umpteenth time. It is for those who are not sure how to get off to a <u>good</u> start.

This book is written to be "an easy to use" guide to finding employment. It is for those job hunters who may have disadvantages in getting their next job; not so much because of who they are, but because of their past. The majority of career books today are written for "perfect" people—those who look good, have college degrees and stable job histories. This book is for those who fall into a less-than-perfect category—too young, too old, not enough experience, too much experience, recovering alcoholics and addicts, ex-felons, welfare mothers, single mothers, homeless, and others. Thousands of individuals have used these tips and gotten the job they were after! You, too, can use this information to create and reach your own success.

If you want to change your life, all you need is the desire to change your life and the willingness to take some advice from people who have "been there, done that." I have worked with thousands of job-seekers, from all walks of life. With determination and a willingness to change, many of them were able to turn their lives around. Here is your chance to learn from their successes.

It would be easier, perhaps, if I could be with you in order to coach you along and answer your questions. Of course, I'm only human and can't be everywhere at once. Still, the information here will help you as you move forward.

This book focuses on how to get a job simply because a job can make turning your life around much easier. You will learn more about how the working world "works"(you may be surprised at how dysfunctional the working world is) and earning money will give you the freedom to do whatever you want in the future.

A NOTE ON STARTING YOUR OWN BUSINESS

Starting a business is another way to turn your life around. However, it is usually easier to get a job than to start a business. It almost always takes money to start a business. It won't cost you a dime to go find work. For those of you who want to start your own business, it is recommended that you get a job so that you can earn money and learn important skills while you are starting your own business.

We will look at the 'secrets' of the working world. Actually, there is one secret that no one will tell you because it is so subconscious that all of us do it without even realizing it! You will be judged according to how you look. This may or may not be legal discrimination. At the very least, it is the act of discriminating between job candidates in order to decide who to hire. If you look clean, people will assume you are clean. If you pay attention to details (belt, ironed clothing, accessories like jewelry and ties), people will assume you are detail-oriented. If you are well-groomed, people will assume that you care about yourself and your reputation. They will then assume that your cleanliness, attention to detail, and care for your reputation will come to work with you and benefit them as well.

Look at it this way…an employer has one job opening and fifty applications to review. From those applications, the employer decides to interview twenty. In order to choose the best person for the job, the employer will use information from the application and results from a 30-minute to 1-hour interview in order to decide who is the best person for the job. Only one of the applicants will actually get the job! That means that even small details can be important in evaluating and deciding who to hire.

Understanding the reasons for employers' attitudes and impressions can help you overcome objections and succeed in finding a job by simply changing your clothes, changing your mind, and changing your attitude! The results of your renewed job search will be up to you. If you do not apply the information, you won't have any results. If you do apply the information, your results will be real work leading to a real future!

Of course, finding that job and creating your future may take time and require patience and persistence. Still, you've made it this far, so a few more days probably won't hurt.

Take a second to look at yourself from the employer's perspective. If you owned a business, would you hire yourself? Why? Why not? Are you dependable? Are you trustworthy? Are you clean and neat? Will you get along with co-workers and customers? *Remember, if the employer does not make money, s/he cannot afford to pay employees, including you.*

The employment process, and this book, can be looked at using five keys for unlocking the successes in your future career/working life:

1. KNOW yourself.

2. KNOW your employer.

3. KNOW your competition.

4. SHOW that you know what you know.

5. SHOW what you know.

Your Future At Work

But, it's not just getting the job that matters—it's keeping it!

We all know someone who can get any job they apply for, right? They wear the right clothes, they say all the right things, and they smile at all the right times. But can they keep that job...? Realistically, most entry-level and re-entry jobs pay low- to mid-range wages and you will need raises in order to increase your ability to support yourself and your family.

You'll earn raises after you've established job stability and a stable work history. So, keep this next job for at least one year before moving on to something better.

THINGS YOU SHOULD KNOW ABOUT THIS BOOK...

• This book is *not* politically correct.

• It is a source of information for you. The results are your responsibility.

• All names have been changed in order to protect those who have been able to turn their lives from bad to better.

• This book is written to inform as many people as possible about what may work in their favor and what may work against them. In trying to answer all of the questions from years of managing employment services agencies and training both job-seekers and job counselors, there is some information that is not relevant in all situations. There are some very specific details in this book; if they are not appropriate for your situation, do not worry about them.

- It focuses on those items that you, the job-seeker, have in your control.

- It talks about the 'unspoken rules.' Still, there is an exception to every rule in here. Unfortunately, it is difficult to know when you can tell 'the truth, the whole truth, and nothing but the truth.' Most of the time, that much truth will not get you hired. Instead, you should tell 'the truth, the *positive* truth, and nothing but the truth.' The goal here is to help you find the positive truth *in employer's terms*.

When Dorothy left Florida, she was running away from an abusive husband and some legal problems. She couldn't afford airfare, so she hitchhiked across the country. She was penniless when she arrived in California.

When taking a second look at what her past revealed, we found that she was persistent (she didn't stop until she got all the way to California) and resourceful (she had no money and yet she got where she was going).

Those two traits, persistence and resourcefulness, which took her out of an unhappy situation in Florida, enabled her to start a new life in California. Employers appreciate persistent and resourceful staff people. At interviews, Dorothy was able to focus on the positive while still telling 'the truth' to prospective employers.

- Employers are human. So are you. We all make assumptions. The only difference is the assumptions we make, because assumptions are based on our personal experiences and every individual has a different set of experiences. In other words, if my only experience with two-headed Fanganians is negative and you are a two-headed Fanganian, then I may make assumptions about you that are negative. Likewise, if I am a one-eyed Grouper and your only experience with one-eyed Groupers is negative, you may make assumptions about me that are negative. We are all human.

This goes both ways. You do not know enough about the employer to know whether he or she is having a good day or a bad day. Perhaps you look like her favorite uncle or his favorite aunt. Perhaps you look like the mother or father (niece, nephew, cousin, you name it) who always taunted him. Most of the time, we do not get jobs for reasons that are within our control. Sometimes, we do not get jobs for reasons that are out of our control.

In turning your life around, try to remember that the world is full of humans. We do not always know why they do what they do. You will be more successful if you just keep moving forward and stop worrying about other people's problems.

THEORY OF REALITY

'This theory emphasizes that reality is not the way you wish things to be, nor the way they appear to be, but the way they actually are.'

'You either acknowledge reality, and use it to your benefit, or it will automatically work against you!'

Ken Masco, Business Management Systems

CHECK YOUR REALITY

This book is about the realities of the employment world. It does not sugar-coat these realities. It is based on numerous interviews with a variety of employers and job-seekers as well as personal experience. It reveals some of the attitudes and biases that employers may have about the people they interview and hire.

The employment world generally believes that the world is as it appears to be. In others words, employers believe Flip Wilson's Geraldine when she said, "What you see is what you get, honey." That fact can, and should, be used to your advantage.

There are many roads to success. If this one appears closed, turn the corner and take another road!

2

Know Yourself

Sounds obvious, doesn't it? But very often, we just don't seem to get it. "But, really, I'll do anything! I just need to make money!" Of course, you'll do anything...for a day, for a week, maybe for a month or two. But, in order to really change your life, you'll do better if you get a job that lasts long enough to bring you benefits, promotions and raises. Also, if you stick with a job for more than one year, it is significantly easier to leapfrog into a better job somewhere else!

There are thousands of different jobs, and thousands of variations on each job. That is why it is so important to know yourself. The more you like your job, the longer it will last, and the easier it will be to start earning more.

There are three things that make showing up for work worthwhile:

1. you actually like the work you are doing;

2. you like the people you are working with; and/or

3. you like the amount of money you are earning.

If you can hit two out of these three, stay put as long as you can. Many people are satisfied with one out of three, but you deserve better. Also, your job performance will be better if you're happy and so you're likely to last there longer.

For example, if you want to become a hairstylist, you can look for work in downtown Los Angeles or in Beverly Hills. Both locations will have the same basic skill requirements. However, they will probably have different pay rates, fellow staff, and clientele. While you may be very well-suited to one location, you might not be comfortable in the other location.

Perhaps, you have strong communication skills and would like to work in sales. You can apply to work at a wide variety of retail stores, like The Gap or Tiffany's.

Again, it's the same job. Still, the difference in the environment makes them very different. If you know where you are comfortable, you can focus your job-hunting efforts appropriately.

There is a job for almost every personality, skill, and preference. It is a question of figuring out what is best for you and working to get it. If you want to wear sweatpants to work, perhaps you should consider working at a gym. If you want to wear jeans, there are many casual industries such as landscaping, construction, and even some sales environments. If you prefer to wear a suit, then you can look for an office position or certain other sales environments. As you can see, your position, your company and the location of your office will all have an impact on whether this job is well-suited to you.

> Did you know that there is a man who is paid to build large Lego installations? Imagine that, paid to play with toys for a living!

FIRST THINGS FIRST

So, what do you prefer? Start with some basic preferences. If you were guaranteed one of two jobs, and both paid the same wages, would you rather…

Be indoors or outdoors? _____

Wear jeans or wear suits? _____

Do physical labor or sit at a desk? _____

Have variety or one single task? _____

Be alone or with others? _____

Be surrounded by quiet or noise? _____

Now, stop and think about what you want in the future. After all, if you don't know what you want, you won't know if you are going in the right direction and you won't know if you get it.

Pause for a minute and ask yourself: What do I want? Do I want a better life for my children? Do I want a car (or a new car)? Do I want a house? Do I want nice clothes, jewelry, travel,...? What do I really want?

Right now, I want:

_____

For most of my clients, this blank is usually filled with "a job." That's fine. Whatever job you get now is a stepping stone. After all, you have a long life ahead and this job probably won't last forever. As a matter of fact, you probably don't want it to! So, what do you want next?

In two years, I want:

_____

This might be a promotion, a raise, a new job. It might be your own apartment, a new car, or something special for your family.

My ultimate goal is:

_____

At first, it may be difficult to think in terms of a timeline. Still, it is rare that anyone gets everything they want all at once. Some people start with college. Others start with an entry-level job. Either way, your next job is not likely to get you rich quick. Hasn't everyone heard, by now, of the man who won big in the lottery but was broke only one year later? For most of us, it takes time to build a career and a bank account. You may not get it right away but if you don't start, you're not likely to ever get there. The opposite is true, too, the sooner you start, the sooner you'll get there!

According to the *Los Angeles Times* (2/15/2002), Richard Cook started his career at Disneyland as a steam train and monorail operator. Thirty-one years later, he was named Chairman of Walt Disney Studios.

Plenty of success stories start at the bottom and move slowly to the top. How about the high-school kid who started as a grill-cook at a fast-food restaurant and is now a restaurant manager or working at the corporate offices? How about the high-school kid who started as a Warehouse Clerk and is now making a six-figure salary selling the same electrical components that he used to stock?

Of course, you may not want to reach the 'top.' After all, the 'top' in a career often means less time with your family. Still, it costs money to raise a family, which makes even an entry-level job a high priority.

First, three tips:

- *You can change your clothes.* When I walk into a room, people look at me and they are thinking that I am trustworthy (or not), pretty (or not), considerate (or not), able to do the job (or not), similar to their customers (or not), competent (or not), confident (or not). My goal, and yours, is to make them think that you are trustworthy, well-groomed, considerate, able to do the job, able to relate to their customers, competent, and confident. All other attributes are related to these. For example, if you are applying to be a landscape maintenance worker, you will look different than an accountant. But you will still need to look trustworthy, well-groomed, considerate, able to do the job, competent and confident.

What job would you like to apply for? _____

What clothing would you need to show that you are the right person for the job?
_____

(i.e. steel-toed boots for construction work)

In reality, when you meet someone new, they probably know nothing about you. You tell them who you are by what you wear, how you act, and what you say. If you look like you looked in the past, people will assume you are still the same person and that you will do the same things. If you change your clothes, you will look like you have changed for your future actions.

- *You can change your mind.* Changing your mind means actually looking at your past in terms of your future. When you tell others about your past, you speak in terms of your future. It doesn't matter what you did in the past. If you are not going to do it again in the future, it should not be held against you.

- *You can change your attitude.* Changing your attitude is changing your expectations and assumptions about yourself and others. If you think your glass is half-empty, people will treat you as if your glass is half-empty and it will continue to be half-empty. If you think your glass is half-full, people will treat you as if your glass is half-full and it will get more full. Likewise, if you assume others are treating you unfairly, you will react to them in negative manner. If you assume the best of others, you will treat them better and get better results. Focus on the positive.

SELF-TALK

How do you speak to yourself? 'Geez, I blew it again! I'm always doing this…' or 'Good enough. I'll do better next time!'

What do you usually say to yourself when you make a mistake?

_____

What is something positive that you could say instead?

_____

When someone compliments you, how do you usually respond? 'What? You think this outfit is attractive? It's an old hand-me-down.' 'You think I'm thin? No, my hips are really fat.' Being aware of your thoughts and reactions can help you get beyond them.

How do you speak about other people and situations? When you compliment them, you mean it, don't you? Yet, for some reason, when others compliment us, we assume that they don't mean it. We all do this! It's because of our cultural upbringing.

Our culture is not always self-affirming. Often, it's considered sophisticated to be negative about ourselves, others and the world around us. Still, most people prefer to be around people who have a positive attitude. Listen to the people around you. Do they look at the positive aspects of a situation or peoples' good qualities? Listen to yourself. Do you say positive things about yourself or the people around you?

Most of us have seen movies about people who decide to change their lives. (Good Will Hunting and The Princess Diaries are two examples.) Some of us know people that decide to change their priorities in life. Often they don't fit in anymore.

Change is challenging. When you change yourself, you change your relationship with the world and the people around you. When you decide to become more successful, you separate yourself from others who do not want to change or are afraid to change their lives. They're used to the _old_ you and it will take time for them to get comfortable with the *new* you. As you grow and decide on different priorities in your life, family and friends may treat you differently. Don't let them stop you from reaching your goals.

Motivational speaker Suze Baez tells the story of her visit to a restaurant in Baja California. In the window was a large, low bowl full of crabs. Several of the crabs were climbing the sides of the bowl trying to escape. A few were almost at the top. She went in to tell the maitre d' that some of the crabs were close to escaping. He smiled and asked her to watch for a few more minutes. The crabs that were below started pulling the escaping crabs back to the bottom of the bowl!

DON'T BE SHY!

'Our deepest fear is not that we are inadequate. Our deepest fear is that we are powerful beyond measure. It is our light, not our darkness, that most frightens us. We ask ourselves, who am I to be brilliant, gorgeous, talented and fabulous? Actually, who are you not to be? You are a child of God. Your playing small doesn't serve the world. There's nothing enlightened about shrinking so that other people won't feel insecure around you. We were born to make manifest the glory of God that is within us. It's not just in some of us; it's in everyone. And as we let our own light shine, we unconsciously give other people permission to do the same. As we are liberated from our own fear, our presence automatically liberates others.'

This important message has been credited to both Nelson Mandela on the occasion of his 1994 inauguration and to Oprah Winfrey. It almost doesn't matter who said it; they are both strong individuals who have overcome the odds of their pasts. And, this quote bears repeating, over and over and over…

NOW is your time to SHINE!

Still, it's important, at this point, to be balanced in your approach to the employment arena, to be both confident and realistic. You are probably still looking at entry-level or re-entry work and wages. Once you get that, and keep it for a year, you'll be in a good position for a more successful future.

A WORD ABOUT CHOICES

Most successful people are big believers in choice. They believe you choose to be who and what you are. While that may seem depressing—'Gosh, did I really do this to myself?'—it should be exciting. It means that you can choose, at any time, to become a better person, to become a different person. You can choose to be a survivor, not a victim. Anyone who is meeting you for the first time does not know about your past. They do not know anything about you, except what they can see. You can start changing your future by changing what people see when they meet you.

Our choices are influenced by any number of things outside ourselves. Things we saw and heard as children, and experiences we have had in our lives. Everything we know came from other people. Much of what we believe is what we have been told by the culture around us—music, family, friends, television, magazines, newspapers, and movies all impact how we view the world and ourselves. Everything adds up to how we view the world and how we expect the world to treat us. All of it is learned and all of it can be changed.

If you were told you are beautiful and smart when you were young, you grew up believing it. If you were told you are stupid and never going to amount to anything, you will believe that too.

Beautiful, smart, stupid and "never going to amount to anything" are all judgments. These are just other people's opinions. They have no basis in who you are. What do you choose to believe about yourself?

For every question, request, comment or opportunity, there are always at least three choices: yes (I agree), no (I don't agree), and compromise. Sometimes, we don't think about our choices because we know we couldn't bear the consequences so it doesn't even seem like a choice. At other times, we don't think about our choices because we've built habits that make simple choices into a daily routine. Knowing that you have a choice can give you power to make your life better.

Samantha, a twelve-year-old whose mother was physically abusive, had to make a choice. Every three months, Samantha came home from school knowing that it was almost time for her mother to 'blow-up.' Samantha would be beaten for any reason at all on those days.

What were Samantha's options? She could run away, become an emancipated minor, or stay in an abusive home. She ended up staying with her mother because she knew that that would enable her to finish school and that education was the only thing that would enable her to build a better life.

Today, because she feels like she made a choice when she was young, she can look at the positive side (education) of growing up with an abusive mother.

3

Know The Employer

When you apply for a job, others are applying as well. The more you know about the employer, the more you can tailor your approach to win the job. For your average entry-level position, this does not actually require additional research. It does require thinking from the employer's side of the desk.

An employer is trying to earn money through a business. Businesses serve customers with products and/or services. In order to have a successful business, it is important to have three things: (1) a quality product/service, (2) customers who purchase the product/service, and (3) a staff which works well together and keeps the customers happy.

In order to accomplish those three things, the employer must hire staff who can be depended upon to do quality work and get along with both fellow staff and customers. If the employer doesn't earn money, he can't pay you.

The boss needs you to do the work…and you need the boss to pay the bills!

Pretend that you're the employer. What would you look for in a job candidate? What sort of person would you hire? _____

_____

_____

_____

DISCRIMINATION

Discrimination is the act of differentiating and deciding between different options. We discriminate when we choose one movie instead of another or one brand of toothpaste over another. Legally, employers cannot discriminate based on certain factors: age, gender, religion, ethnic background, disability, political affiliation, sexual orientation (depending on which state you work in). However, it is possible to discriminate against someone based on these factors while still appearing to be legal in hiring the "best candidate for the position." It is too bad that this kind of discrimination still exists today. Happily, in many ways, things are improving. Among others, technical experts, such as computer programmers, are making strides in this area. However, if you don't have those strong technical skills and, sometimes, even if you do, this topic is still an important fact of life.

For the most part, employers may preach diversity, but many still practice discrimination, in one form or another. Much discrimination these days is actually based on social or economic factors, rather than ethnicity factors. Still, there are four basic reasons that employers discriminate:

First, in order to select the best candidate for the job, the employer must decide between different individual's strengths and weaknesses in terms of the job. Often, employers only have one job opening, even though there are many job applicants. From 20 (or 50 or 100) applicants, the employer must choose the best *one*.

Additionally, an employer wants to hire someone who will "fit in" with the rest of the staff. For example, if everyone who works in the shop is the same gender and ethnicity, it is often easier to hire someone new of the same gender and ethnicity, so as not to 'rock the boat.' While it is not fair and is potentially illegal, these employers are typically concerned with staff morale which is a legitimate workplace concern. You, as an applicant, should recognize the logic here. If everyone else in the office speaks Spanish and you don't, even basic communication may be a daily challenge.

Perhaps, they have had a negative experience in the past which influences their decision. For example, there are some employers who are veterans of the Vietnam War. They might not want to hire a Vietnamese employee based on their personal negative experience in that country. This is unfair and illegal discrimination; however, it is often difficult to prove in a court simply because there are so many factors that contribute to the hiring of an employee. Additionally, would you want to work in an office where you are unappreciated because of your cultural background? Probably not.

Also, an employer may have formed opinions based on stereotypes which are the result of peer influences, television, movies, and a lifetime of input from various sources. There are two ways to look at any individual; as a matter of fact, there are two ways for any individual to look at themselves and to represent themselves. If you are age 55, you may be 'old and inflexible' or 'mature and experienced.' An employer might prefer an employee who is mature and experienced but would probably not hire someone who is old and inflexible. Stereotypes often contribute to these sorts of attitudes. However, you may contribute to these attitudes as well. If you are aware of potential stereotypes based on your age, gender, ethnicity, religion, etc., you can dress in a manner that will downplay or contradict those stereotypes. In the example above, a job candidate in the upper age ranges would do better to be wearing clothes in bright colors that reflect well on him/her and current or classic styles that fit well, not too tight and not too loose. Old clothes will make you look older. Also, hairstyle can make you look older or younger. Women can look older or younger by using cosmetics to their advantage [hint: more cosmetics are not usually better]. Only you can decide. Are you old and inflexible...or mature and experienced? Are you young and immature...or eager to learn? It's your choice. It's all in how you frame your experience.

You can change your clothes...

So that you do not appear as an employer expects and thus beat the stereotype.
You can change your mind...

So that you speak as you would like to be seen and not as the stereotype would be seen.
You can change your attitude...

So that you assume the employer's intention is for the best...and not the worst.

Now, even while you assume that the employer is not discriminatory, you want to know what stereotypes are out there, and how to beat them, so that you avoid any possibility of discrimination and present the best, and most employable, you.

The Value of Education

There is a definite value to having a strong education. On the other hand, education can be over-rated. I've known college graduates earning only $10 per hour and can point to United States presidents (most notably, Abraham Lincoln) as well as millionaires (Dawn Steele, Tony Robbins) who had only a high school diploma or GED. There are as many roads to success as there are definitions of success.

From the employer's point-of-view, experience and attitude are even more valuable than education. While school can teach you some basic skills, it cannot teach you habits that are important for keeping your job: being on time, working consistently all day, getting along with customers and co-workers.

Sometimes, individuals go to school because they are avoiding the inevitable…getting a job! Unfortunately, few of us are paid while we are in school, which makes it difficult to afford rent, meals, and raise a family. Getting a job, however, can enable us to pay for what we need and then we can attend school on weekends!

The Value of Preparation

There are some activities that will help you prepare on a continual basis for the interview process. These activities will help by surrounding you with professional people and potential employers as well as career/work-related images and ideas. They are not free, but they are inexpensive. And, remember, many things that are worth something, also cost something.

- Toastmasters International is an organization with local clubs all over the United States. These clubs are designed to improve your public speaking and personal communication skills. I know several individuals who doubled their income within one year of joining this fine organization. Call 1-949-858-8255 or visit their web site at www.toastmasters.org to find a club near you. If you don't like the first club you visit, try another until you find one that works well for you.

- Read magazines that focus on professional activities: *Time, Newsweek, Working Woman, Working Mother, Forbes, GQ,* and *Inc.* are all useful magazines. Also, magazines are less expensive if you subscribe. If you like the magazine and have a dependable address, it is worth the investment. They are also available to read for free at the local public library.

- Watch some videos that will help you visualize the differences between various living and working environments. Some good ones include: *My Fair Lady* with Rex Harrison and Audrey Hepburn; *Six Degrees of Separation* with Donald Sutherland, Stockard Channing, and Will Smith; *Working Girl* with Melanie Griffith, Sigourney Weaver and Harrison Ford. Additional movies that will show you the difference that your image can make include *Princess Caraboo* with Phoebe Cates, *The Associate* with Whoopi Goldberg or *Long Kiss Goodnight* with Geena Davis and Samuel L. Jackson.

What You Can't Change: Stereotypes: Ethnicity, Age, Gender

Changing your ethnicity is impossible. Black, brown, olive, white (or African-American, Hispanic-American, Asian-American, European-American)…there are stereotypes attached to all ethnic backgrounds. Some stereotypes carry advantages, some carry disadvantages. It is important to know which stereotypes and attitudes may be held by those whom you would like to influence.

Let's put this in perspective. If I walk into the room and you see that I am Caucasian (white), 25 and female, you will have an immediate impression of what I can or cannot do for you. Likewise, if I am white, female and 50, you will likely have a different opinion of what advice I may have for you. These opinions are based on stereotypes. Perhaps you will listen to the 25-year-old as if she were your daughter or your sister. Perhaps you will listen to the 50-year-old as if she were your mother or your aunt. If I want you to respond to me as a professional businesswoman with valuable information, then I must make sure that other aspects of my appearance gain your respect and attention.

If I were to send my male colleague (either the 25-year-old or the 50-year-old), you would probably have two different opinions…before either of them had a chance to utter their first word.

Additionally, how you respond to me is specific to who you are. Men might respond to me one way, women might respond yet another. Your age will also influence your responses.

It is important to remember that most stereotypes are based on media images which are, as often as not, incorrect. However, they are the images that fill our collective minds and influence our snap judgments. Stereotypes are also based on previous personal experiences. For example, were I harassed or raped by a Marine, I might be predisposed to thinking poorly of Marines. Likewise, had my life been saved by a Marine, I would probably think very highly of Marines.

What You Can Change: Skincare, Cosmetics, Wardrobe, Hairstyle

No one likes to think that they are judged according to how they look the first time they meet someone. However, they all admit to judging someone else the first time they meet. This is how we know that image matters. Some sources go so far as to say that the first impression is formed in less than 40 seconds, the secondary impression in 40 minutes and it takes 40 encounters to change these initial impressions.

There is an advantage to this. If you are ready to change your life and take the next step to success, you can do so by simply adjusting your look. A new hairstyle, a new suit…and you can change how people see you.

Your adjustments should still reflect who you are. Keep in mind that you are seeking work that you will like. Are you applying for a job at Denny's Restaurant or at a fancy restaurant in Beverly Hills? Dress accordingly.

Color

John Molloy's <u>Dress For Success</u> books spend a great deal of time talking about the impact of color in business situations. It is valuable information that can be boiled down to some basics.

If you are applying for office and career positions, conservative colors will typically serve you best…brown, gray, and blue, in the dark and medium ranges. Red can be worn very effectively by women. If a man wants to wear red, it should be in his tie (or he risks looking like Santa Claus!). Women interested in higher level positions should avoid prints and patterns. Solid colors will make you appear stronger.

Look (Weight, Figure, Wardrobe)

It is not necessary to go on a diet just to get a job! Still, it is important to look your best no matter what you weigh. That means that your clothing should fit you well, not too tight and not too loose. You should tuck blouses/shirts in and wear a belt. Remember that you can wear a business jacket that will hide any extra 'love handles.' It is always better to be overdressed than underdressed. After all, you can always take off your jacket but, if you don't have one, you can't borrow one once you get to the interview.

Jane Darling had a weight problem. She knew she was overweight but couldn't seem to drop the extra pounds.

Finally, she went out shopping one weekend and bought a new wardrobe that was two sizes larger than her old wardrobe. When she went to work on Monday, all of her officemates asked if she had *lost* weight! Why? Because the new, larger clothes fit better and looked better, too.

Your wardrobe should be professional, classic or current, and should fit your body well. We can hide a multitude of figure flaws with the right clothing. If you are unsure, you can go window-shopping at an upscale department store (i.e. Nordstrom, Macy's or Robinson's-May) and get advice from the clerk. You don't have to buy anything and you will get information on what colors and styles flatter you. Go back when you get your new job and buy something then!

If you are looking in magazines for ideas, it's important to choose the right ones for your purposes. Magazines such as *Seventeen* are appropriate for young people who want to work in youth-oriented businesses. If you are older and are looking for an office position, then *Working Woman* or *Working Mother* might be a better choice. For more conservative industries and companies, *Forbes*, *GQ*, or *Inc.* may be the proper magazine.

Once you get the job, there are two items to remember. First, the initial 90 days on the job is considered a trial, or probationary, period; you should err on the conservative side. Second, you'll want to decide whether you are dressing to 'fit in' or to 'move up' in the company. The most easily recognizable example of the difference between these two dressing styles is that of female staff members in an office environment. Usually, when the office gets cold, the secretaries put on sweaters and the managers put on business jackets. Perhaps you want to strike a balance by having both a sweater and a business jacket handy so that you have a choice.

Hair

Early in my career, when I had just been promoted from an Assistant position to a Training position, I was asked by an older male colleague why I still had "secretary hair!" At the time, I didn't even know what that was. Now, when I enter an office I look at the women working there and consider the differences. Many of the secretaries and assistants do indeed have long hair. The managerial women usually have short or shoulder-length hair. Those that have long hair tend to wear it up and off their shoulders.

Put Your Best Face Forward

For the Woman…According to several studies, women who wear cosmetics earn more money than women who do not. While it is not fair, it appears to be true. Women can look younger or older by applying makeup correctly. One suggestion: Less is better and looking natural is better. It should never be obvious that you are wearing cosmetics and that you are trying to look different than you really are.

For the Man…Good skincare is essential. Wash your face regularly. If your skin is dry, use a moisturizer. If your skin is oily, use an astringent to keep it clear.

The beauty industry is a multi-billion dollar industry for a reason and don't think it's just women who make it that way. Men have been known to spend beaucoup bucks on hair replacement as well as plastic surgery (you're just not likely to see them buying foundation at the drugstore)!

If someone mentions this, listen!

There are some items that are considered very personal and that most people will be reluctant to mention. Either (a) it is not that important (to them anyway), or (b) they do not want to risk offending you or losing your friendship, or (c) they are male and feel it is inappropriate to mention to a female and/or risk a sexual harassment lawsuit. The following items are of the utmost importance to you! If someone says it is a problem, it probably is and no one else has the guts to tell you! Do something now!

* Halitosis (bad breath) * Bad body odor * Dirty hair *
* Need to wear a bra and/or pantyhose * Visible nose hair *

What You Can Choose: Economics, Past History, Attitude

Attitude (as evidenced by…)

You can probably tell when your friends are upset just by looking at them. You may even be able to tell how they are feeling over the phone. People can pick up cues based on voice, facial expression, posture and body language. Your attitude is often conveyed based on verbal and physical cues.

...FACIAL EXPRESSION

Rule #1:   SMILE! People would far prefer to work with someone who is positive. There is more than enough negativity in this world.

...POSTURE

Rule #2:   Stand up straight! Sit up straight, too. People with high self-esteem tend to have good posture. Additionally, good posture will make you look taller than you look when you are all hunched up.

...BODY LANGUAGE

Rule #3:   Use open gestures instead of closed gestures. For example, avoid pointing with your finger. Instead, use an open hand. Do not cross your arms across your chest.

From the Bottom Up...

"You can pull yourself up from anywhere as long as you have one good outfit, stand up straight and wear it with a smile." Said innocently enough at a luncheon, the woman next to me thought it encapsulated the beauty of the problem. You really can get the job by looking good. You'll gain the "smarts" you need to keep it as you go!

A WORD ABOUT MOTHERS AND ENTRY-LEVEL JOBS

Despite media reports, most employers are not family-friendly. If a family-friendly workplace is important to you, go to the library and look in *Working Mother* magazine, and ask them about other resources to find companies that have family-friendly policies. Still, that does not mean a company will hire you because of your children. *Employers hire people to do work.*

Many employers have had experiences with mothers, especially single mothers, who they believe paid more attention to personal priorities than to their work. Therefore, when given the choice, an employer will usually hire the person without children. For this reason, I recommend <u>not</u> telling the interviewer/employer about your children during the application/interview process. After all, they are interested in your ability to do the job, and your children should have no impact on that.

More specifically regarding this matter, there are three things that mothers of children, especially young children, usually do that employers do not like. They (1) spend time on the company telephone during work hours talking to their children, the babysitter, the doctor, the teacher; (2) arrive to work late because it took them extra time to get their children ready for the day's activities; or (3) they are out sick often because their children are sick often.

Once you have a job, it is important that you be aware of both your children's needs and your employer's needs. After all, *if you are keeping your employer happy, you will earn more money which will enable you to better care for your children.*

Later in this book, there are specific recommendations for dealing with questions regarding children that may come up in an interview.

"I hate to reinforce a stereotype, but give me another."

4

Know Your Competition

This section should actually be called 'you don't know your competition.' Perhaps, the others competing for this job are just as bad off as you, or worse. Perhaps, they are also ex-felons, or welfare mothers, or limited English speakers. You don't know.

You do know YOUR qualifications for this job. You can cook, drive, answer telephones, learn quickly, type, be on-time every day, whatever is called for. When you are interviewing, focus on your abilities and qualifications. You can even tell the employer, 'I don't know who else is interviewing for this position, but I do know that you can depend on me to do a good job every day.'

Also, remember that you know very little about the interviewer…You do know that s/he currently working, and that s/he will determine whether you get hired, or called in for a second interview.

5

Show That You Know What You Know

This chapter is the longest chapter in this book. It is not necessarily the most important. Still, employers will generally make assumptions about what you can (and can't) do before you get to prove how good you are. Likewise, everyone brings something different to the interview and to the job. This chapter covers the most detailed information for the widest variety of job-seekers.

I CAN CHANGE MY CLOTHES

This section is about the first impression you make, whether it's when you walk in the door or call for a phone interview. Your first impression to others includes your cleanliness, grooming, and clothing. It also includes your written presentation; specifically, your application and/or resume.

FIRST IMPRESSIONS COUNT!

Once they know your name, your first impression has started!

The interview begins when the potential employer has your name. If you give your name over the telephone, then the interview has begun. If you give your name when you walk in the door, then the interview has begun. All too often, we think that the interview begins when we step inside the office of "the boss" or of the Human Resources representative. However, in today's competitive job market, all levels of communication may have input in the hiring decision. Put bluntly, you don't know who's sleeping with whom. This primer will prepare you for all aspects of the interview, from the initial telephone call to the follow-up letter.

Several employers I've interviewed have regularly asked their receptionists for notes regarding applicant behavior over the phone and in the lobby. Someone applying for a customer service job who did not treat the receptionist politely would not be expected, or trusted, to treat their customers or their co-workers politely.

Additionally, the receptionist can always 'lose' your message before it even gets to the interviewer. Your potential employer may never even know that you called!

In order to get a job, you need to start looking like you are already employed. While it is possible to get a job if you are unemployed; the old saying is still true: It's easier to get a job if you have a job. An employer will assume that, if you are currently working, you are a good employee and are worth hiring. You need to visually show an employer that you know what they need from you when you arrive at work every day. You want the employer to 'see' you in the job as soon as they meet you.

The First Impression

The very first thing that people will notice is how you look. Generally, they will simply do a visual appraisal (as you probably do when meeting someone for the first time). Very often, how someone is dressed or their body language will give strong indications of personal and professional habits that can have impact on an individual's performance. It is at this time in a relationship that we often decide whether or not we like and/or trust a person. If you want them to hire you, it is important that they like and trust you.

In terms of your visual image and physical appearance, there is a rather long laundry list of items that are basic and that everyone should pay attention to. Some of you will undoubtedly smile at the particulars in this list. Please keep in mind that this list was compiled through experiences over years of managing employment services agencies for a *wide* variety of clients. If it's here, I've seen it done! *By following these guidelines, you will increase your chances of getting hired because you will look more professional.* Yes, there may be an exception to any rule. Rules, however, are based on the odds…and, odds are, this list will serve you well.

- DO SMILE.
- DO walk with upright posture (poised, yet relaxed).
- DO stand up straight, chin up.
- DO look the employer in the eye.
- DO dress appropriately for the job applied for.
- DO wear colors that look good on you and clothing that fits nicely.
- DO wear moderate jewelry, or none at all.
- DO wear clean shoes that match your outfit and are appropriate to the job for which you are applying.
- DO—WOMEN—wear moderate makeup.
- DO have clean fingernails that are no more than 1" long. WOMEN—DO wear light or conservative nail polish (i.e. clear or pale pink), or none.

- DO—MEN—be clean-shaven or keep your beard/mustache close-clipped.

- DO tuck in your shirt and wear a belt, even if you are overweight. It will give you a polished and finished appearance.

- DON'T wear perfume or cologne. (Allergies are more common than you think).

- DON'T wear flashy fashion jewelry. DON'T wear nose, tongue or lip rings.

- DON'T wear wild nail polish colors like red, black, white or neon.

- DON'T wear clingy polyester or tight spandex outfits.

- DON'T wear miniskirts or halter tops that will make others wonder what position you are applying for.

- DON'T wear bold/heavy makeup (NO blue or green eye shadow).

- DON'T wear more than two rings or bracelets per hand.

- DON'T wear an extreme hairdo.

- DON'T wear baggy clothing.

- DON'T wear flashy ties with a Hawaiian print or broad flowers.

- DON'T slouch.

- DON'T frown.

- Oh, yeah…DON'T look at the floor or at the ceiling or at your feet and DON'T fidget.

You want to look confident. You want to look your best. It is okay to be yourself, but it must be done in a tasteful manner so that you do not appear cheap or trashy or inappropriate to the company culture. Yes, there are exceptions to these rules, but not many.

There is a hotel in Orange County, California, that will not hire female maids if they do not come to complete the application in a dress. For this hotel, it is important that all employees know they are hotel representatives. If you don't represent yourself well while looking for work, they doubt that you will know how to represent them once working with their guests.

Some readers may be on a tight budget. It doesn't matter. You can look good on any budget, it is a matter of knowing what to spend your money on (no matter how much or how little) and then doing so. Even thrift stores have a wide variety of choices.

Standing and walking with good posture will imply self-confidence. If you are confident, the employer will have confidence in you. Looking the employer in the eye will further imply that you are interested in them, their company and the position. Smiling will imply that you are good-natured. If they are going to spend 20-40 hours a week with you, they certainly want you to be good-natured!

Looking For Work

People will begin wondering about you as soon as you make your first contact, whether it is over the phone or in person. This section will focus on telephone interviews and how to dress for your first contact.

Be aware that once the employer has your name, they are making decisions about you. Are you nice? Clean? Friendly? Professional? Should they spend more time considering you for this position? This primer will help you complete your application so that it rises above the rest and keeps yours at the top of the pile! If you are still at the point in your career that you must complete an application before the interview, read this. If you have been completing dozens of applications but not getting interviews, read this.

First, you will want to find job leads so that you are applying for jobs that are already there. It is easiest to get a job working for someone who needs you. Though, if you read Richard Bolles' What Color Is Your Parachute?, you will learn about designing your dream job and getting hired to do it. Not a bad idea, but it does take time. It's probably more practical for you to get a job so that you can be earning money while you are designing your dream job!

Still, the more focused your job search is, and the more well-suited you are to the job, the easier it will be to convince the employer to hire you. Why? Because you really do want the job and will be a stable employee.

Jerry Goffin, with his wife Carole King, wrote 60's hits such as 'Locomotion' and 'Will You Still Love Me Tomorrow?' He wrote songs after work while employed at a chemical plant. It was several years before his dream became a reality. He held on to his dream while supporting his wife and family. Even if you are a single parent, you can support your family and continue working on your long-term goals and dreams.

Get your job leads where you will. Many jobs are found in the classifieds (yes, believe it!). Even Frank Stein, a regional product manager for a medical equipment manufacturer (earning more than $100,000 per year), found his position through an ad in the newspaper. Some job leads are found at college bulletin boards, in the windows of stores, or through associates at networking organizations or just by letting friends (from church or elsewhere) and family members know that you are actively looking for work. Nowadays, many jobs can be found in listings on the internet.

It's best to look for jobs that you think you will like. If there is a store where you currently shop, or wish you could shop (if you could afford it), see if they have an opening. If you like cars, consider working at a gas station, or as a mechanic, or at a car dealership. If you like sports, look for a sports store, or a sports magazine publisher. There are always a variety of jobs in any business <u>and</u> a smart employer would rather train someone with enthusiasm (if they learn quickly) than hire someone who has no energy to do the work that needs to be done.

Where do *you want* to work? What do you enjoy doing? Talking with others (customer service, sales)? Cooking (restaurant)? Driving (taxi, delivery/courier, truck)? Gardening (landscaping)? List your top three job choices here:

_____

_____

_____

Commonly, once you have a lead, you will need to:

- Telephone,

- Apply in person, or

- Send your cover letter and resume by mail or fax.

If it is not listed in the ad, you want to call first and get the name of the company and the name of the person in charge of hiring for this position. If the ad only provides a fax number, fax a resume with a cover letter. Many ads will provide a phone number or address. If not, you can always use the phone book to look up the phone number if you have the name of the company. Then, ask the receptionist, 'Who is responsible for hiring for this position?'

This way, you can personalize your letter of interest more than the competition. By personalizing your letter, you will gain more favorable attention. (Think about it: Doesn't it feel good when someone calls you by name? Wouldn't you open a letter addressed to you before you would open a letter addressed to 'Resident?')

The Telephone Interview

Consider what you can tell about your friends during telephone conversations. Can you guess whether they are enthusiastic or depressed, angry or relaxed? Of course, you can! Well, the person on the other end of the line today will pick up the same clues from your tone of voice. Here are a few hints to make sure your telephone image is the best it can be. Prepare for the phone interview as if it were an in-person interview. Dressing as if you were going to their office will help you feel more professional, even on the phone. Having your resume and/or application at hand will allow you to answer, without hesitation, any questions that you weren't expecting.

- DO dress well.
- DO smile.
- DO speak clearly. Before you make the call sit with your feet flat on the floor and take three deep breaths. It will relax your vocal chords and help you speak more clearly.
- DO be prepared with your resume or completed application.
- DON'T mumble. If they can't understand what you are saying, they may not ask you to repeat yourself. This is especially true if the job entails working on the telephone (receptionist, secretary, telemarketing).
- DON'T slouch.

Typically, it is after the phone call, that you will be asked to visit the office in person—either for an interview or to complete an application. So…

Be a Boy Scout: Be Prepared

With any luck at all, you will be hired today! Be prepared for the best. Who knows? Maybe their best staffer just ran away with the cook. Bring a pen so that you can complete an application. Bring two kinds of identification (i.e. driver's license, social security card, birth certificate or passport, green card). Bring transcripts, certificates, awards, recommendations and anything else that will prove you are as good as you say you are. Bring an extra resume (fax copies just aren't the same).

Also, bring a pre-prepared application so that if you are asked to complete an application, you have all the dates, addresses, phone numbers, and names that you need in order to be thorough. Remember, neatness counts. If you complete a thorough and readable application, they may not check on the details. However, if you leave details off of your application, they will assume that you are hiding something. I know several people who leave the high school section of applications blank. They are correct that an employer is not likely to check on the high school status of an adult applicant; however, if it is blank, the employer will wonder what was going on during high school (drugs, alcohol, runaway, delinquent, etc.). Don't give the employer a reason to question. Remember the other applicants for this job are "perfect." They remember their high school. They may even cite various activities during that time such as sports, drama, or academic honors.

Being prepared will show that you are an organized, thoughtful, and detail-oriented individual.

Applications come in a variety of shapes, sizes, formats and questions these days. Some companies actually use an application that is in the computer and you type your answers. Some applications are old and ask questions that are illegal by today's standards. For example, it is not legal to ask your age or date of birth; still, if a company is using an old form, it may be there. If it is, you probably want to answer the question.

You should go to the corner market or a store at the local mall and ask for an application (preferably two). You're not necessarily going to apply there though you can if you want to. However, you should create a 'master' application which you can bring with you for completing applications elsewhere. Use the following tips for creating the best possible 'master.'

APPLICATIONS

General Rules

It is important to remember that if you lie on an application, you may not be hired *or* you may be fired when the employer finds out that you lied. Even if the employer does not fire you immediately, they will know that you are not trustworthy (after all, you did lie) and it will be harder for you to get promotions and raises. In this section, you will find some artful and creative suggestions that may provide you with an effective way to avoid a difficult situation. It is your choice whether or not to use any of the tools mentioned here.

- DO fill in all blanks. If there is no answer, put N/A or—.

- DO look for blanks along the side of the application. Fill those in, too, unless marked "Office only."

- DO be honest. DON'T lie.

- DO bring current identification (Driver's License [preferably for the state in which you are seeking work], state identification card, social security card, military identification card, passport, green card).

> Jane Clemens was very nice and had strong clerical skills. She had just moved to California. She came to me after several weeks of job-hunting.
>
> Because she was still using her Utah driver's license as identification, employers didn't want to hire her. They were concerned that she was planning on moving back to Utah.

REMEMBER: Employers use the application to learn about you *and* about how you communicate on paper. The application represents you when you are not there to represent yourself.

Personal Information

- DO write down the name that any roommates may know you by as well as your legal name. It seems basic, but even a nickname like "Jimmy" can be noted. Just write, James "Jimmy" Jameson.

Back in college, Cassandra completed an application with her legal name only, Cassandra Lee Case. However, her roommate called her 'Justin,' which was short for Justin Case. Unfortunately, when an employer called for Cassandra, her roommate forgot her real name. The employer thought she had the wrong number and Cassandra didn't even get the message.

- DO use your current address. If it isn't your home, use the address but don't mention the name of the agency/friend that is helping you. It's important to have an address, even a Post Office Box. Otherwise, the employer will question your stability and the employer wants stable employees who will be dependable.

- DO use your voicemail number. It is not necessary to provide your work phone number if you are currently employed. Most employers will understand that you do not want to receive calls at your current job.

NOTE: You should, if possible, use safe phone numbers. If you do not have a phone of your own and are using a friend's phone or an agency phone to receive messages, ask them to be careful not to mention that you don't live there. They should say, 'Joe isn't available right now. I'll make sure he gets the message when he gets in.'

Additional Information

- DO write down who referred you (if applicable) or how you learned about the job. Employers spend money on advertising open positions, and they want to know that their money is well-spent. Also, where you learned of the job will tell them whether you know someone that they already trust, whether you read the newspaper or whether you are a regular customer.

- DO specify the job desired. DON'T write "anything." Employers want to hire individuals who are well-suited to the work. If you write "anything," they will assume you are well-suited for "nothing." You can, however, be vague (General Office, General Maintenance, General Production, Retail/Office, etc.)

- DO write a start <u>date</u>. "ASAP" is rarely accurate. Specifically, if you say "ASAP" and are asked to start tomorrow morning (because someone quit today and they need you immediately), it will look bad if you respond with, "Well, I'm not really available until Monday." Just put Monday's date on the application in the first place. Or, if you are currently employed, write "2 weeks from date of offer." A smart employer will respect your desire to give adequate notice to your current employer.

- DO write "open" or "negotiable" for salary desired. Or, if it was indicated in the ad or by your contact, write the range that the employer is planning to pay. This will let the employer know that you are aware how much (or how little) s/he is offering and that you are willing to work for that amount. Research what similar jobs are paying.

> Several years ago during a job interview, a friend of mine was asked what she was expecting to be paid per hour. She responded with a specific number, only to have the employer laugh and tell her the bottom of the pay scale was 50 cents per hour more than she had asked for. It is no better to underbid yourself than to overbid.

- YOU MAY write "no" when asked about contacting a present employer.

- DO let the employer know what skills you have. Make it easy for the employer to want to hire you by telling the employer how much you are able to do. As a matter of fact, take a moment RIGHT NOW to make a list of EVERYTHING that you can do. There are employers for almost every skill. Can you drive (Delivery)? Are you good mechanically (Auto Repair)? Can you cook (Cook, Chef)? Can you balance a checkbook (Bookkeeping, Accounts Receivable/Payable)? Can you get along with others (Sales)? Be easy on yourself at first. Be open. And don't take your skills for granted. You may be surprised to learn that things you've done for free your whole life are actually marketable job skills.

- Look closely at any volunteer or community service activities that you've done.

> Charlene Jenkins, a homemaker who had raised five children, thought she had 'no experience' working outside the home. After spending more time with her, she mentioned that she had been the Treasurer of the AYSO soccer league and President of the PTA. This, with a list of other committee work she did, created a resume reflecting strong skills in organizing and managing people, time and money.

Education and Abilities

- DO use the last grammar/high school you attended in the appropriate blank. This is important if you attended several schools.

- DO put the name of a school in at least the open "High School" blank. You may be saying to yourself, "I'm 45-years-old. Why does it matter what grammar/high school I went to?" Good question! It doesn't really matter, but employers tend to assume that everyone who was clean, sober and stable while they were growing up, will remember the name of their old schools. As a matter of fact, if you can read, write and fill out the application, most employers will believe that you graduated from high school. If you do not remember the name of your grammar school or high school, you may want to write George Washington Elementary School or Thomas Jefferson High School in the blanks. Some names are common for grammar/high schools and, if you are old enough, look honest and have some work experience, it is not likely that an employer will call to check your old school record. If you leave it blank, the employer will wonder, 'Why is this blank?' Perhaps because you moved a lot as a child (unstable) or perhaps because you were drinking or using drugs (irresponsible). There is no reason for you to be held back because of choices that your family made for you or a past that should be left in the past. *It is not necessary* to put in the year of your high school graduation. If you are over 40, you do not want to put in the year of your high school graduation. Just write yes or no. If you have a GED, write GED instead of no.

- DO speak in the most positive terms you can while still being honest. If you did not complete high school, write that you completed ninth grade or tenth grade or eleventh grade. Let the employer know what you *have* done, not what you haven't.

- DO include Regional Occupational Program (ROP) classes for trade school education, whether you completed the course or not, as long as you learned the skill.

- DO use the current name of the school, not the old name. For example, if you live in Orange County, California, you may have attended Santa Ana College. Now, it is actually two schools: Santa Ana College and Santiago Canyon College. Use the current name, if you know it.

- DO use a major subject in college or use 'general education.'

- DO use all of your background: hobbies, volunteer work, community service, General Relief work, etc.. Often, the application will ask, 'Is there anything else we should know when considering your application?' Since you want the employer to like you better than the next applicant, this is your opportunity to give them a reason. Even if it is as basic as 'I am a regular customer.' They will appreciate knowing that you are interested in their products and their work.

Work Schedule

- DO complete any questions regarding limitations on your work schedule. Speak in positive terms. Tell the employer when you are available, not when you are not. Many people will say 'NOT AVAILABLE AFTER 9 P.M.' because the local busses are not running after that time. The employer does not need to know that. The employer needs to know when you *are* available, 'AVAILABLE BETWEEN 7 A.M. AND 9 P.M.'. Likewise, many parents will say, 'NOT AVAILABLE AFTER 5 P.M.'. It is better to say, 'AVAILABLE FROM 8 A.M. TO 5 P.M.'. Be honest about the hours you are available. It won't do you any good to say that you are available at all times and be scheduled for a graveyard shift. If there is no way for you to get to work at that time or if the residence in which you live requires that you be 'home' at night, then you will have to tell the employer that you're not really available. Then, the employer may be less interested in hiring you for the day shift either! Employers do not appreciate it when they are told one thing, 'I CAN WORK AT ANY TIME,' and find out another thing, 'I CANNOT WORK AT NIGHT.' You yourself probably do not appreciate it when someone says they can do something for you and then, when you ask them to do it, they say, 'Oh, I can't really do that.'

The Questions

- DO read the questions on an application carefully before you put an 'X' for an answer. One 40-year-old client checked 'YES' to the question, 'ARE YOU UNDER 18?' Well, when the employer is reading your application, there is a good chance that you are not even in the room. The employer will have no way of knowing that you really are over eighteen. Because minors are governed by laws regarding working conditions, you may not want to be mistaken for a 17-year-old. Likewise, some employers prefer hiring minors because it enhances the atmosphere they are promoting. Then, it would be to your benefit to be under eighteen. Either way, it is important to pay attention to the details of the question and be honest when you answer.

- DO you have any physical condition or medical concern which would limit your ability to do this job? First of all, if you are truly not physically capable of doing a job, I recommend that you look for work that is better-suited to you and your abilities. However, having worked with differently-abled adults, it is obvious that many individuals are very capable, given enough enthusiasm and determination as well as the right job.

> Everyone liked Jamie because she was so friendly. Unfortunately, no one really wanted to be too close to her for too long. She was taking a medication which gave her an unbearable body odor problem. Still, she had bills to pay and needed a job.
>
> Her happy ending: Jamie was hired by a perfume manufacturing company where no one even noticed!

Be honest on this question but keep in mind that there are many sicknesses that will not interfere with your ability to do the job. Here are some examples.

First of all, anti-depressants, taken regularly, will not limit your ability to do the job and the employer has no need to know. Check NO.

Diabetes, if cared for properly, will not limit your ability to do the job and the employer has no need to know at this time. Check NO. If you have had a diabetic episode, you should inform the employer's medical officer or personnel office in case of emergencies, but notify them after you've been hired.

Epilepsy, if medicated, will not limit your ability to do the job in most cases. Some jobs are particularly high stress (i.e. ambulance driver) and create an increased chance of epileptic episodes during critical times. Consider carefully the position you are applying for. Also, after you are hired, you should inform the medical officer or personnel department. You want them to know what to do in case of emergencies.

- HAVE you ever been convicted of a felony? If you have been convicted of a felony, you have three choices: lie, leave it blank or check YES and explain. You can lie, but it's not recommended. Often, you get caught in this lie and you will, more than likely, be fired. You can leave it blank. Some employers won't even notice, especially if they are busy. You can check YES. Your decision may depend on the actual conviction and the circumstances surrounding the crime (or non-crime, if you are still claiming to be innocent). In the explanation section, you should then note the actual Penal Code of which you were convicted (for example, PC 69) and 'will discuss in interview.' This will let the employer know that you are now being honest and allow them to check what crime you committed if they are interested. It will indicate that you are willing to answer questions regarding your conviction in the interview. The interview will be covered in another section.

If you were convicted of a drug crime, you should be aware that, while a majority of Americans have experimented with drugs at one time or another, most employers do not want to hire drug-users. If you say YES, make sure to indicate your willingness to undergo drug-testing before being hired. Many employers automatically do drug-testing anyway. One employer I am aware of uses the hair-testing method which, reportedly, can tell whether you've used drugs within the last six months! You may also indicate how long you have been 'clean.' Do not go into details on the application.

If you were convicted of burglary, do not expect to get a job where you will be responsible for property or handling money. Some employers will still hire you but most are not going to risk you stealing from them. However, if the circumstances surrounding the burglary were limited, you may be able to get a second chance.

If you were convicted of kidnapping (which is becoming more common given the increasing divorce rate and custody battles), you may find an understanding employer. On the other hand, you may not.

In any case, if you talk about your past as if it is your past and not as if it is your future, you will probably be able to convince someone to hire you and give you a second chance.

- DO you have reliable transportation? There is only one correct answer to this question: YES. No reasonable employer would hire someone who cannot commit to being at work, reliably, every day that they are scheduled to work. You either walk, ride a bicycle, ride a bus, or drive a car. If your car is unreliable, try to find a job within walking distance of your residence—particularly if you are considering minimum wage jobs, which barely pay enough to cover your rent and food bills, much less the cost of gas or bus fare. This question may also come up in the interview, especially if you do not look like you own a car.

Experience (Employment and Otherwise)

- IF you do not have actual paid work experience, you may complete this section using volunteer work, community service hours or school experience. The purpose of this section is for the employer to gather information about your interests and your work habits as well as your trustworthiness.

If you're still young, under 20, and looking for your first job, it is perfectly acceptable to use information about extracurricular and high-school activities like sports, drama, and clubs.

Lying on the work experience section of an application is discouraged! One client who was looking for work in California actually wrote that he was currently working for his uncle on the East Coast. It was nice to know that his uncle would lie for him but how do you work for someone on the East Coast while you live in California? In this age of virtual internet telecommuting, it is certainly possible but not very likely. Find the positive way to look at the truth in your life and in your work/education/life experience.

One woman, Katie, had been in prison for ten years. She had a choice: She could lie and make something up, pretend that she had been unemployed for the past ten years, or say that she worked for the Serious City Federal Penitentiary. She chose the latter. Here is an example of how her entry looked:

From (Mo/Yr) 02/78 To (Mo/Yr)   05/88   Salary: Room and Board
Company   Serious City Federal Penitentiary
Address   1 Repentance Lane, Serious City, CA 99999
Telephone Number   (123) 456-7899   Supervisor Mr. Big Jerk
Reason For Leaving   Better Opportunity   Title and Responsibilities
Office Assistant: Responsible for filing, distributing uniforms and making license plates.

Future employers at least know that she is being honest about where she has been for the last ten years. Of course, this option should be used only if you have lost the most recent ten years of your life due to incarceration.

- DO have accurate information about past employers and past positions (address, phone number, salary, dates). If you must, look it up in a telephone book. Even out-of-state telephone numbers are available by going to a large library or calling Information. They are also available by looking on the internet.

Typically, the most difficult part of completing the experience section of the application is remembering the dates when you worked at those old jobs. Here are some ways to refresh your memory: (1) Work backward. When did you hold your last job? The job before that? (2) Start from high school. 'Let's see…my first job out of high school was…' And so on. (3) Think of other important events in your life and match your work dates accordingly. For example, if you got your first job after the birth of your first child, or after your parents passed away. It's probably easier to remember significant personal events than work dates, so this can work well. Whatever method you use, it will be easier to get your next job if you can fill in the blanks regarding your past jobs. Once you fill in your 'Master' application, you can bring it with you when you go to fill out applications with employers.

Reasons for Leaving

- DO consider your reasons for leaving past employment.

  - SAY "RESIGNED" instead of "QUIT".

  - SAY "DISCHARGED" or "LAID OFF" instead of "FIRED".

  - SAY "RELOCATED" instead of "MOVED".

  - Use "goal change" or "personal considerations".

You want to avoid looking unstable and establishing any patterns in this section. You still need to tell the truth. However, if you say that you have left your last three jobs in less than three months because you 'RELOCATED,' then the employer will not hire you because s/he (wisely) is wondering how soon you will move and leave this job. If you have been 'LAID OFF' once, it is okay. If you have been 'LAID OFF' three times, you will be considered 'deadwood' and are not likely to be hired.

If you left your job because of abuse, you should look for another reason. Many employers do not want to know about your personal life. Certainly, you do not want them to know that much about your personal life. However, at the time you left your job because of abuse, you probably also 'RELOCATED' to another (safer) living situation. Simply say, 'RELOCATED.' You do not have to say where you moved (even if it was only one block)(and definitely not if it was to a shelter).

If you left your job because of pregnancy, you should look for another reason. Many employers do not want to hire young mothers. They fear that mothers will be late to work (because they have to prepare their children for school), sick (because their children are sick), or on the telephone often during the work day (talking with children, teachers, doctors, etc.). It is better to look at your life and, if you went back to school during or after your pregnancy, say 'RETURNED TO SCHOOL.' If you moved during your pregnancy, say 'RELO-CATED.'

There are two ways to look at everything…

One of the biggest challenges in the EXPERIENCE section of the application arises when you have had a number of jobs in the recent past, i.e. three to five jobs in the past year or two. Unless you are still a student, that is usually frowned upon by employers. With good reason. They have work to do. It is time-consuming and expensive to hire and train new employees. If you have held that many jobs in the past year or two, it looks as if: (A) either you are not a good enough worker to be worth hiring, or (B) as soon as you are trained, you will probably leave. Now, of course, your goal is to get a job that you are both (A) good at, and (B) planning to stay at. You will need to convince this employer of that.

- DO include employment-related references such as employers, teachers, coaches, counselors, and/or parole officers. After all, just because you know someone in a certain profession, doesn't mean you were their client. Just because I know several parole officers, does that mean I've been on parole?

You may also want to attach a resume to your application. Whether you fill out an application or not for employment, having a prepared resume shows the employer you are a serious job-seeker. It also helps you organize your experience and education and other pertinent information.

This workbook has been written for job-seekers at the beginning of the career ladder. Many times, entry-level employees are not expected to have resumes. However, it is always good to have a resume. It can help you organize your work experience and skills in an easy-to-read format. There are many well-written books showing a wide variety of resumes; so, here are just a few pages showing you the basics and giving you some suggestions that may help you. Remember, many of the books on the store shelves are written for "perfect" job-seekers with high school diplomas, college degrees, extracurricular activities and a stable work history. You can use a resume to show *only* the best of yourself, which can be very much to your advantage.

Preparing A Resume

You will need this information:

- Your name, current address and current telephone/voicemail number.

- Work Experience: include company names, job title, dates you worked (month/year) and a job description.

- Education: include Regional Occupational Program (R.O.P.) training, vocational schools, seminars, college degrees/coursework. Do NOT include high school.

- Certifications: include certificates, awards, professional memberships.

- Foreign Language(s): Are you bi-or tri-lingual?

- Travel: U.S. and foreign.

- Hobbies: What do you do in your spare time? Do NOT include religious or political activities.

IMPORTANT: Remember that a resume does not replace an application. Unless you are told to do so by the interviewer, it is NEVER appropriate to write 'please see resume' on the application.

Your resume should have a neat, clear format so that employers can find the information that will entice them to hire you. Try to get the important information on only one page. The only job-seekers with a two-page resume are seeking $50,000 or more. Watch out for typos. Do a spell check. Have someone else proofread it. Make sure you give out only clean photocopies. Make sure it is organized and use parallel construction (all items should be arranged in the same way). Please see the sample resume on the next page.

SAMPLE RESUME

I. WANNA JOB
1 Nokidding Lane, Hallelujah, CA 77777
(111) 111-1111

PROFESSIONAL EXPERIENCE

The Golf Club, Irvine, CA, 6/90–7/93

> Responsibilities included customer service and retail sales of sports apparel as well as processing cash, check and credit card payments at this exclusive boutique for female golfers.

Hotel for Homeless Women, Santa Ana, CA, 9/92–5/93

> Responsibilities included case management, group counseling, crisis intervention, telephone referrals and resource counseling for shelter residents. Promoted after six months from Assistant to Lead position.

Senior's Point Retirement Community, Irvine, CA, 9/91–12/91

> Responsibilities included case management, assisting in activities and group leadership for elderly adults.

EDUCATION

> A.A. Rodent Psychology, Rancho Santiago College, May 1988.

TRAVEL

> United States (Maine, Florida, New York); Mexico; Canada.

LANGUAGE

> English, Spanish.

PROFESSIONAL AFFILIATIONS/VOLUNTEER ACTIVITIES

> Toastmasters International.

REFERENCES Available Upon Request.

Now that you have completed the application, there are several more steps to go through before you are offered the position. These steps are covered in detail in the following pages.

1.   You will be interviewed.

2.   You should send a thank you letter after the interview.

3.   In most cases, the employer will check your references after the interview. At this time, the employer may also check your criminal history and your credit history. These 'background' checks are becoming more common in today's job market.

4.   There may be a second interview with the same interviewer or with another staffer. If no one calls to schedule a second interview or offer you the job, call them the following week. Ask if they've made a decision yet and, if not, offer to come in for a second interview. Employers do keep applications on file. I have even received calls for interviews (which lead to job offers) as much as six months after applying for certain positions.

5.   After a second interview, make sure to send another thank you letter.

And, of course, the JOB OFFER!

I CAN CHANGE MY MIND

In order to convince others that you are as good as they want you to be, you may need to change your mind about your past. This will be most apparent in the actual interview, where they will ask you questions about why they should hire you.

First, before we talk about the interview, let's think about who you are. Is there anything in your past that you'd like to erase? _____

Now, is there a positive way to look at it? What did you learn from the experience? Remember, my friend who found resourcefulness and persistence in her escape from Florida? What's the positive side of your story?

_____

_____

Okay, now let's talk about the interview in detail. First of all, interviews go both ways. You are trying to decide if this job will work for you. After all, you want to work there for at least one year. If you can't fulfill the responsibilities of the job, say so. It is better to find out the job does not fit your life situation before you agree to go to work. Remember—you are also interviewing the company to find out if it fits your needs. Save yourself and the interviewer time. Your honesty may not get you that job but they may remember you for another position later.

Professionalism

It is easy to get lazy when there is no one other than our children, our spouse or our friends depending on us. Your job in the interview is to impress someone who you do not know. This is your chance to show and tell…the good things, not the bad. Remember to:

- Go alone to the interview.

- Arrive 15 minutes early. Often, you will be expected to complete an application. If that is necessary, do so using your pre-prepared 'Master' application. Otherwise, take this opportunity to look around the office. Is it formal or casual? If this is Friday, watch out! It may be the only casual day of the week. Look at any industry magazines on the coffee table. Look at any company brochures. Familiarize yourself, as much as possible, with the business.

- Introduce yourself to the secretary or receptionist. It is possible that the person at the front desk is actually the boss…or has more knowledge about the company (knowledge that you can benefit from). Either way you look at it, your goal is to be hired, therefore you may soon work with this individual. Make friends now…not later!

- Be seated if a chair is offered and maintain your posture as if the interview has already started.

- DON'T take children, relatives or friends with you.

- DON'T gossip or discuss your problems with office personnel (even if you know someone). You don't know who chats at lunch with whom. If you offend the wrong person at this point, you've shot yourself in the foot. Secretaries and other staffers are an invaluable resource in the interview process. They may tell the interviewer what they thought of you and what you were like, both in the lobby and on the telephone. That information can be used for you or against you. The more professional you are, the greater the chances that it will work to your advantage. One never knows where the real power lies.

Body Language

Equally important, once you meet the interviewer, you must establish confidence in your ability to do the job. Here are some basic rules of thumb:

- Shake hands firmly with the interviewer(s).

- Look the interviewer(s) in the eye.

- Use the interviewer(s) names.

- Notice your surroundings and find common interests. Discussing common interests will put you both at ease and help you establish a relationship. However, if you spot a photo of their children, don't mention yours. In most companies, employers aren't looking for staff with competing priorities…and your children could be considered a competing priority.

- Give a firm handshake. Don't give a 'limp fish' or an 'arm wrestler' handshake.

- Make eye contact when shaking the employer's hand. Americans, at least, have a tendency to mistrust those who won't look them in the eye. Trust is an important part of the employer/employee relationship. Establish it early. Additionally, sunglasses can be a hindrance in this area. Once you are indoors, make sure you take your sunglasses off.

- Don't stare. This isn't a contest. It's an interview.

- Don't touch items sitting on the interviewer's desk. This might 'invade their space.'

- Don't accept offers of coffee, cigarettes or anything else. 99.9% of the companies in the United States are now non-smoking. Don't let them know you smoke. As for drinks and food, there is nothing more awkward than being asked an important question immediately after filling your mouth.

A firm handshake, eye contact, and remembering the interviewer's name will let the interviewer know that you are interested in them and that you will be a cooperative employee.

Be a Boy Scout (Again): Be Prepared

You are now going to represent yourself in person! So, all of the details mentioned before come into play here as well. Yet, there's more. Some of these items seem obvious; however, since we're (me, too!) usually nervous before an interview, let's just go over them together.

What's the Point of the Interview?

The employer wants to know if you will get along with your boss and your co-workers. That is one of the largest reasons for an interview. It is easy to tell from an application, assuming the applicant has told the truth, whether or not some-one is capable of doing the job. If I need someone who can type 90 wpm, I can easily figure that out from reading the application. However, it's equally important that my typist get along with other staff. If not, I may find that the typing gets done but that nothing else does.

The employer may also consider the job duties as well-suited to an extrovert or an introvert. For example, if you are applying for retail sales, the employer may be looking for and expecting to hire an extrovert. Indeed, it is important for you to think about the job duties and whether or not you are well-suited to the position. *The employer wants to make sure that you're going to like this job enough to keep it.*

Scent

- DO have a 'fresh' deodorant smell.

- DO shower and wash your hair.

- DO have clean, fresh breath. Brush your teeth. (DO NOT drink coffee or smoke after brushing).

- DON'T wear perfume or cologne, just in case the interviewer is allergic.

- DON'T have smoker's breath or a smoke smell on your clothing.

- DON'T have bad breath in general.

- DON'T chew gum. (Throw your gum away before entering the building).

Some interviewers may be allergic to smoke, perfume or cologne. Moreover, many offices in the United States are non-smoking. Also, a potential employer will worry about how many smoking breaks you would take. Finally, strong scents are an immediate turnoff to an interviewer.

Types of Questions Employers May Ask (and Why)

Why do we even have interviews? Employers want to know that you can not only do the job but also will get along with fellow workers and customers. They have only your application/resume and a short interview to determine this.

Employers know nothing about you unless you tell them. Likewise, you know nothing about them until they tell you. This can be either good or bad. What it means is: DON'T ASSUME ANYTHING! Even though, as you have seen already, the interview process is full of assumptions. You don't know if the interviewer is an abusive husband, an abused wife, a weekend drug user, a Vietnam vet, or even an ex-felon.

Also, don't be too 'chatty.' Even though employers want to know as much about you as possible, you need to protect yourself from misuse of information by not telling them, for example, that you have two young children, are a recovering alcoholic/addict, have been living in a homeless shelter for 45 days and if you don't get this job will be asked to move back on the streets. *They want to hire you to do work.* Most employers will give donations if they're feeling charitable, they will not give jobs. They give jobs to people who can stay focused on getting the work done. In the interview, stay focused on what will impact your work performance and leave your personal life where it belongs…at home!

More than anything else, chatting can get us into risk of being discriminated against. This is when we let it slip that we grew up in the fifties (age), have young children (mothers), have past lifestyle problems (drugs/alcohol/abused). Employers do not want to hire employees with major weaknesses, real or imagined. If an employer is asking about your taste in music, he/she may be trying to determine your age or your lifestyle choices (i.e. Do you listen to Bill Haley and the Comets, Tony Bennett, or Snoop Dogg? Amy Grant, U2 or Garth Brooks?). Of course, if you're interviewing for a job in the music industry, that *is* a relevant question, isn't it?

That being said, when answering questions, remember that life experience, not just work experience, counts! If you have little paid work experience but have volunteer or hobby experience that applies, make sure you mention it. For example, if you are a female applying for an auto mechanic position, and you grew up with three older brothers and were always helping fix their cars, it's helpful to mention it.

It's best if you can answer questions in complete sentences. Interviews can be uncomfortable for employers as well as for you. Going beyond 'yes' or 'no' answers will help establish a conversational, and more comfortable, atmosphere.

How can employers be uncomfortable in interviews? After all, they have all the power! Well, it's like this...The employer has only one job opening. S/he is interviewing twenty people. S/he has to decide which one person can have the job and which nineteen are 'out of luck.' It is not fun to have to tell nineteen people that they didn't get the job.

General Overview Questions

An employer wants to know that you have the basic qualifications to do the job.

Answer general questions *positively* and truthfully. Any question that is similar to, 'Why should we hire you?' falls into this category and is *very* important. If you don't know why they should hire you, they won't spend any time trying to figure it out for themselves. I have actually heard of one employer that starts the interview with that very question. If the applicant doesn't have an answer, the interview is over.

Before the interview, think about your strengths. Are you experienced? Friendly? Resourceful? Enthusiastic? Dependable? Can you type 50 wpm? 70 wpm? Use a jackhammer? A forklift? What are your strengths? When asked a general question, you should answer by saying, 'Because I am...' or 'Because I can...'

My personal work-related strengths are _____

_____

Personal Information Questions

The employer may be concerned with your personal life to find out if there are interests that you have in common, or to discover potential work-related problems. Some of these questions are legal, some are not. Either way, they may be asked, especially if you are interviewing for a small or family-owned business where they may not be familiar with employment-related laws.

- If you are asked about your children, the employer is probably trying to find out whether or not you will have child-related concerns which will keep you from your work (i.e. late to work, making/receiving calls, out sick due to sick children, etc.). While it is not legal to ask these questions, they often relate to legitimate employment-related concerns. Your goal here is to let the employer know that work is one of your highest priorities (after all, without work it will be difficult to support your children).

- If you are asked about your marital status, the employer may be trying to evaluate your stability, your moral code, your availability for dating, or your availability for business travel. It is illegal to ask this question in an interview situation. It has nothing to do with your ability to do a good job. Respond with something such as, 'This job is my first priority and I am available full-time/over-time/for travel.'

- If you are asked about your spiritual beliefs, an employer may be trying to find out if you have that in common, your moral code, or if there are any religion-related work concerns (such as requiring Saturdays or Sundays off). Questions about religious beliefs are not legal to ask in interview situations. Again, spiritual beliefs usually have nothing to do with your ability to perform a job, unless you are applying at a religion-related business; in which case, your beliefs will at least have an impact on how well you will get along with your co-workers.

- Remember that while some employers are "good guys", others are not. It is best to keep the interview focused on the job and your ability to do the work, not on your personal life. Just because an interviewer is interested in your personal life, does not mean that they will hire you once they find out the 'dirt.' I have seen several clients tell personal stories during interviews about the stress in their personal lives (one actually mentioned that his young child had died), only to find out that they didn't get the job. Because there are so many people looking for work on any given day, the employer can always find a legal and legitimate reason why they hired the other applicant and you will never know whether or not your 'sob story' got in the way. Generally speaking, you want to tell the employer about your strengths, not about your weaknesses. Personal stressors should be classified as weaknesses and kept private.

Answer these questions by focusing on your commitment to this job. For example, 'It sounds as if you're concerned about my commitment to this job. Let me assure you that this job is my highest priority.'

Questions Regarding Authority

The employer wants to see if you can work well under his/her leadership. Do you work better when you are told what to do, or if you are allowed to work alone? How good are you at giving directions to others?

Answer these questions by indicating that you are able to work well with others as well as on your own. Most employers today desire flexible employees who can think independently but still perform in a team atmosphere. Some positions are more independent, others are more team-oriented. Try to apply for positions that are best suited to your personality in this area.

Questions About Previous Employment

In an interview, never speak poorly of a previous employer. The interviewer often expects that you will bring negative experiences to a new job. S/he is interested in knowing both about your skills-related work history and your people-related work history. Employers may believe history repeats itself. What is your history like?

Answer these questions by focusing on the positive aspects of previous jobs. If you must, admit that you were young and immature at one time, but you have grown since then. Everybody makes mistakes, but you should indicate that you have learned from yours.

Have you 'burned your bridges?' Fortunately, past employers are limited in what they can say about you to a potential employer. If called, they can only answer questions that can be confirmed by fact. Your start date was such-and-such, your end date was so-and-so, you took 364 sick days and you are (or are not) eligible for re-hire. Still, many calls regarding recommendations from previous employers are telephone conversations and, as such, it is difficult to prove what was (or was not) said.

Often, you can find out what your previous employers are saying about you by having a friend call, representing themselves as an employer, and asking about your work habits.

Compensation Questions

The employer wants to know that you will be content to earn what s/he is able to pay. If you are asked directly, 'What salary do you expect?' Respond with a question—'What are you willing to pay someone with my skills and experience?' Or, 'I read in your ad that you are planning to pay between $8-10 for this position, I'm certainly willing to start at that wage range.'

Pressure Questions

Everyone hates to be under pressure. The point of some questions is to see how well you deal with pressure, or how well you deal with the unexpected.

One company's college recruiter asked, 'Why didn't you bring us any doughnuts?' How's that for a pressure question from left field? Take a deep breath, then answer calmly. One person's answer, 'I did bring doughnuts. But I ate them all on the way over.' Unfortunately, there is no one correct answer for these types of questions. Still, if you've prepared yourself in the other areas that this book recommends, it should help you to survive even the pressure questions.

I CAN CHANGE MY ATTITUDE

Attitude is the thing that tells optimists that the glass is half-full while pessimists think that the glass is half-empty. Attitudes are developed throughout your life-time; they are the result of childhood and adult experiences. They become a part of your sub-conscious. ATTITUDES CAN BE CHANGED!

Most of us say negative things to ourselves a lot of the time. "What a dummy!" "Who would do a thing like that?" We say these things without even thinking of them, consciously. But make no mistake about it, whenever you say something negative to yourself about yourself, you help cement a negative attitude in your own mind. *THESE* ATTITUDES CAN BE CHANGED!

Our attitudes become most apparent in the interview when we are answering questions, after the interview while we are waiting to hear whether we got the job, and in how we deal with learning the new job and meeting our new co-workers. All of these may be stressful situations and, therefore, our negative attitudes will sometimes show up, whether we want them to or not.

What attitudes? "I shouldn't have to do all this work just to get a job." "Don't they know how good I am? I mean, just look at me!" On the flip side, we may also be thinking, "Why would they hire me? I don't know nothin'!" Neither side of this debate is a good one. The reality is that as long as there is one job and twenty people (or more) who want it, you will have to work to show that *you are the one* who should get it. They don't know how good you are. As a matter of fact, they don't know anything about you. You will have to tell them. Remember that this is a good thing because they also do not know how bad you are. You will not tell them that.

As for why they should hire you…because you are friendly, resourceful, dependable, responsible, easy to work with, a quick learner, detail-oriented, whatever applies. Professionals know this. Those people that are already making good money know this. They work to get whatever job they want but they also know that any smart employer will want them because they are worth the money.

In order to start changing your attitudes, start talking to yourself in terms of the positive. Positive self-talk is most effective first thing in the morning and right before you go to bed. Write down positive things about yourself and your life. Cursive handwriting (not printing) and speaking out loud will create a neuro-linguistic connection with your sub-conscious mind. This will increase the rate at which your attitudes become more positive. By making the decision to read this book and work with any counselors who may be helping you, you have already started changing your attitudes and your life. Now is the time to keep it up.

There are many good books on positive thinking and affirmations. Go to the library or bookstore and pick one that appeals to you. Read it every day. Recommendations? Many successful individuals have read Think and Grow Rich by Napoleon Hill, Success Is Not an Accident by John G. Kappas, Ph.D., and Get What You Want! by Patricia Fripp.

This next section will help you understand, more specifically, employer attitudes, possible new ways to look at and present your past, and the aspects of changing your life that come after the interview. Once you start accomplishing things in the work arena, you will be surprised at the "domino effect" that you'll see in other areas of your life.

The Interview Questions

In this section, you will learn:

- specific questions which are often asked in interviews,

- information which will help you create your own answers,

- possible answers,

- and reasons why employers ask these questions.

- Then, you will have space after each question so that you may write down possible answers that will work for you.

This way you can be better prepared in future interviews. Remember, practice makes perfect! After you have answered these questions for yourself, have a friend ask you these questions so that you can practice your new positive and honest responses.

Why do you want to work for our company?

- "Because your company is the best in this industry, as far as I can tell."

- "Because I live just one block away and I prefer to work close to home."

- Let the employer know that there is a good reason for you to work at this company. If you are applying at Burger King, say that you like flame-broiled burgers. When you go to apply at McDonald's this afternoon, say that you like their french fries best.

_____

_____

_____

_____

_____

Why should we hire you?

- Usually, when I ask a client this question for the first time, they answer, "Because I need the job." An employer won't hire you because you need a job. For that matter, everyone they're interviewing needs a job. They will hire you because you can do the work, reliably.

- "Because I'll work hard for you. I'm a dedicated and dependable employee."

- "Because I'm an enthusiastic worker and will keep this an enjoyable workplace while doing a good job."

- There are many things you can say about yourself here. I am…resourceful, talented, responsible, always on time, etc. Let the employer know about your work-related strengths, skills and experience. It is not recommended that you say you are perfect for the job. No one is truly perfect.

_____

_____

_____

_____

_____

How is your previous (work) experience applicable to the work we do here?

- There is no cut-and-dry answer to this question. It depends entirely on who you are and what you've done in the past. Let's just say that your answer should tell the employer that you know enough about the job to do quality work and to take care of the customers. Use any experience from your background that is applicable, including fast food, hobbies, and volunteer experience.

_____

_____

_____

_____

_____

What is your experience in supervision?

- "I have no experience in supervision. However, if that is part of my responsibility, I'm sure that you will 'show me the ropes.'"

- "When I worked at McDonald's back in high school, I was promoted to floor lead after only six months of part-time work. It was not extensive supervision, but it allowed me to understand the challenges of being boss."

- "I was the team captain for the swim team back in high school. I wouldn't call it supervision exactly. But it gave me some experience with leadership."

- "I was Floor Lead at Joe's Air Parts Warehouse. I had a crew of five, and was responsible for scheduling shifts as well as training and time off."

_____

_____

_____

_____

_____

What did you like best about your last job?

- "I liked working with a wide variety of people."

- "I liked working independently."

- "I liked the variety of work that I was given."

- "I liked the focus of my work."

- Try to determine which aspect of your last job applies to the position which you are applying for and use that for your answer.

_____

_____

_____

_____

_____

What did you like least about your last job?

- "I actually liked everything about it. I would have stayed, had I not moved."

- "I didn't like being indoors at a desk. That's why I'm applying for this more active, outdoors job."

- Avoid saying negative things about your last job. You may find out, after you've answered the question (and it's too late), that what you said you hated was actually a large part of the job you were interviewing for. On the other hand, if you hated filing at your last job, now is the best time to find out that it is a large part of this job, too. Maybe you don't want another job that involves filing (or whatever).

- If you are applying for a position that is significantly different than your last job, it is appropriate to indicate that you didn't like whatever (say, office work), and that is why you are applying for the opposite sort of work (say, landscape maintenance).

_____
_____
_____
_____
_____

Why do you want to leave your present position?

- "I'm hoping to work for a better company with a strong reputation for quality."

- "I'm looking for a job that is better-suited to my skills and abilities."

- "My friend, Joe Schmoe, tells me wonderful things about this company."

- "I've been looking for an opportunity for advancement and I believe this is it."

- Whatever you say, do not say anything negative about your current job or employer. Focus your answer on why this company, or job, is better than your current company, or job.

<u>Does your employer know you are planning to leave?</u>

- "No, and I'd like to keep it that way until I'm able to give notice. In fairness to them, I will need to give (one or two) weeks notice."

- "No; however, if you would like to check a reference from them, I do have the name and number for one of my associates that is familiar with my work there. I can give it to you right now, if you would like."

- "Yes, and they are supportive of my search for a better position."

<u>Why did you leave your last job?</u>

- "My employer and I agreed that I would be better-suited to a different type of work. That's why I've started looking for work that is different from what I used to do."

- "I realized that my job there wouldn't serve me well as I got older. So, I started reviewing my skills and abilities in terms of the job market. I believe that I'm best-suited to this type of work."

- "I relocated."

- "I returned to school where I have since earned a Certificate in Microsoft Word for Windows."

- As stated earlier, NEVER speak poorly of a previous employer. Try to focus on other reasons why you may have left a job. If you must talk about a problem with a previous employer (perhaps because you were fired and this interviewer may call), speak reasonably about a mutual disagreement and a positive resolution.

_____

_____

_____

_____

_____

Why did you move?

- "I prefer the weather here."

- "I prefer living in the country (or city)."

- "I wanted to be closer to my family."

- Avoid making statements about negative or personal reasons for moving, such as leaving an abusive marriage, or following a military husband. These have nothing to do with your ability to do the job and may cause an employer to doubt your skills or commitment to the job. Be general.

- Unless this is a temporary position, the employer is concerned about you leaving this job. It costs money to hire and train staff so employers want to hire good people that will last a long time. Also, the employer may be trying to find out if there are any personal life issues that will get in the way of you doing a good job (for example, maternity, abuse, alcohol, drugs). Avoid talking about these things.

_____

_____

_____

_____

_____

Would you be willing to bring us your school transcripts or a DMV printout?

• "Yes. I would be happy to bring you whatever you need by the end of the week."

• This should give you enough time to get whatever paperwork the employer has asked for. If you can get it to them sooner, then you should do so. If you cannot get it for them, then tell them so. But, they will wonder why you can't and if you are hiding some information from them (or lying).

_____
_____
_____
_____
_____

Do you have objections to a psychological test?

• "No, I'll be happy to take a test if it will convince you of my ability to do the job."

• Your answer should both convince the employer that you are reasonable and willing to work within the company's guidelines.

• Some companies have been "burned" by employees that are not psychologically sound. Extreme examples of this include the shootings of bosses and co-workers at various companies. Psychological testing is something that employers do to protect themselves, their current employees, and you.

_____
_____
_____
_____
_____

What is the biggest mistake you've ever made?

- "Not keeping my first job for an entire year. I was young then and, now that I'm older, I feel a greater desire for stability."

- "Not starting college right after high school. However, I have since taken a variety of courses at junior colleges and trade schools."

- "Not completing college. However, I do value the experience that I had while I was there, and the experience I've gained while working."

- Make sure that you indicate that you've learned from your mistake. Do not talk about mistakes in your personal life, such as abusive spouses or teen pregnancies.

- The employer is wondering if you are human enough to be honest and humble, but wants to hire someone who is wise enough to learn from her/his mistakes.

_____

_____

_____

_____

_____

Have you ever been fired from a job? Why?

- "No. All of my previous employers have been sorry to see me leave."

- "Unfortunately, yes. I was much younger and immature at the time. Now, I intend to make you a very happy employer by being productive and dependable."

- Employers want to hire good employees. If you've been fired in the past, it indicates to them that you were not a good employee. If you were fired, be honest but refer to the incident as something in your past and tell them of your intentions to improve your future work. If there was a disagreement with your previous employer, you may simply want to state that the two of you made a mutual decision for you to find employment more suited to your skills and personality.

_____
_____
_____
_____
_____

Why have you been unemployed for so long?

- "I took some time off to think about my future. Now, I'm looking forward to reaching my new goals."

- "I've been traveling throughout the state (or United States). I have friends and family all over and felt that, since I was between jobs, I could take the time to see them."

- "I wanted to be able to concentrate on my studies at Alphabet Banking College. Now that I've completed the course with flying colors, I look forward to applying my skills to work for you."

- "Unfortunately, I made a very bad choice and have been paying my debt to society. I honestly hope you'll give me chance to get back on my feet and live a legal lifestyle." [Note to ex-offenders: If you worked or took classes while serving your sentence, you should refer to those activities].

- Employers want you at work on time (or a few minutes early) and clean and neat. You should indicate you were doing something fairly respectable and responsible with your time and, mostly, that this job will allow you to work hard for them. Do not refer to maternity or injuries. Many employers are reluctant to hire young mothers because of the reasons mentioned earlier. Employers are scared of recent injuries because Worker's Compensation Insurance claims are very expensive and, if you have recently been injured, you may be easily injured again and file a claim against them.

_____
_____
_____
_____
_____

What jobs have you held in the past?

- This question can only be answered by you. Briefly talk about your work history. If you have no work history, talk about any volunteer or community service work that you have done.

- The employer is interested in knowing more about your skills, interests, and abilities as well as your work habits.

_____

_____

_____

_____

_____

Why have you changed jobs so frequently?

- "I have been spending time learning about the work world and how I best fit in. I now know where I want to be and that is why I am applying here."

- "At first, it was because I didn't know what to do with myself. Of course, given the variety of work I've done, I've finally figured out where I want to be. That's why I am applying for this job."

- "The jobs I have held recently have been part-time and so I have changed jobs in order to better my part-time income. One of the reasons I am applying for this job is that it should allow me to take care of my financial obligations with only one job. So, I'll be able to be more stable."

- If you have truly changed jobs a lot (more than five times in two years), this can be one of the most challenging questions to answer. Your answer should indicate that you have figured out what you want to be doing and that you are planning to stay at this job for awhile. You may want to specifically mention how much you are looking forward to working for a company where you can be committed and put down some "roots." Also, remember that it is not necessary to put all of your past work experience on your application, especially if you have no gaps. For example, if you had several overlapping part-time jobs, you may want to leave one off of your application so that it will not come up in the interview.

- Employers want to hire and train dependable employees who will work hard for them for long enough to make it worth their money. If you have changed jobs a great deal, an employer may think that you are not planning on working for them for very long.

Please give me your definition of the job position you are seeking.

- "The description I saw for this position is perfect for me."

- "I am looking for an entry-level position in a reputable and growing company like this one."

- Target your answer to suit the position for which you are applying.

- The employer is trying to make sure that you will like the job enough to stay there for awhile.

If you were to start all over again, what field would you enter?

- "You know, I'm really not sure. I'm just starting out and it seems important for me to get a good grasp of the basics. I'll make my decision after I have more experience."

- "This industry is really where I want to be, that's why I've applied here. With life expectancies what they are nowadays, it's never too late to start a new career."

- This question is designed to see whether or not you are interested in the position/company for which you've applied. If you are just starting out, you can get away with the first answer above. If you are older, you should use some variation of the second.

_____

_____

_____

_____

_____

Have you ever thought of going into business for yourself?

- "I have. But I prefer the stability of working for others."

- "No. I like the benefits of working for someone else."

- This question is designed to see if you are planning on leaving the job anytime soon to start your own business. Whatever you say, you should indicate that you plan on sticking around for while.

_____

_____

_____

_____

_____

Why do you want to change fields now?

- "I've worked in a variety of jobs and have discovered that this field is best suited to my skills and experience."

- "Whenever I look at the future of the business world, this industry seems to be where the future lies. I want to get in on the ground floor."

- With this question, the employer is trying to determine whether you will stay in this job for a long time or not. Employers do not want to hire someone who will quit quickly. So, they try to determine whether or not you will like what you are doing.

_____

_____

_____

_____

_____

What brought you into this field?

- "All of my previous work experience has led me in this direction."

- "I wanted to use the skills I learned and loved while I was growing up."

- The employer is trying to find out if you are serious about this business and will hold on to this job for awhile.

_____

_____

_____

_____

_____

Have you had any serious illnesses or injuries?

- "No, I haven't."

- "Nothing that will prevent me from working hard for you."

- If this job will be bad for your health and physical well-being, you should not be applying for it. For all jobs, these answers are what the employer wants to hear from the employee to be hired.

- If you were injured at your previous job (or had an epileptic or diabetic seizure), there is a possibility that it will come up when the employer is checking your references. If that is the case, you may want to mention it as if it were a small thing so that you cannot be accused of lying.

- The employer does not want you to get hurt on the job, partially because you are being hired to do work and if you are injured you won't be doing work. Also, because Worker's Compensation is very expensive and the employer does not want his/her premiums to increase. Prior injuries increase the risk of future injuries (at least as far as employers are concerned).

_____

_____

_____

_____

_____

How long are you planning to stay with our company?

- "Realistically, I'd like to commit to at least two years with this company. If it works well, it would be nice to stay even longer."

- The employer is again wondering whether you will leave the job quickly or not. Employers actually spend a great deal of time trying to figure this out.

- However, employers also know that this job probably won't last a lifetime, especially if it's considered entry-level or re-entry. So, saying that you'll be there forever might sound insincere.

_____

_____

_____

_____

_____

What do you see as the most difficult part of this job?

- This will depend on the particular job that you are applying for. Usually, it is best to indicate that you like all aspects of the position. However, you may refer to "more challenging" parts of the job.

_____

_____

_____

_____

_____

Describe your ideal working environment.

- "I really haven't found my ideal working environment yet. That's why I am talking to you. I think this company may be my perfect match."

- "I definitely enjoy working outdoors in the sun and near the water. That's why I've applied for this position at the beach."

- By now, you may be realizing that most interview questions are designed to find out if this job is well-suited to your personality. This is another one of those questions. Your ideal working environment should be similar to the one in which you will be working at this company. For example, if you are applying for a fast-food position, your ideal working environment should be fast-paced and team-oriented.

_____

_____

_____

_____

_____

How did you help to increase sales and reduce costs at your past jobs?

- "I was always creating a pleasant atmosphere for our shoppers."

- "I was never directly involved in the bottom-line, but I try to keep a happy attitude because I know that staff morale can have an indirect impact on customer satisfaction."

_____

_____

_____

_____

_____

Do you prefer working with words or figures?

- "I've always been good with numbers."

- "I actually won my sixth-grade spelling bee. So, I would have to say that I am better with words."

- "To tell the truth, both words and figures are equally important in this kind of work and I try to be good at both."

- Your answer should imply that you are strongest in whichever skill is most important in this position. Or, that you are balanced in these areas.

_____

_____

_____

_____

_____

What did your co-workers think of you?

- "They loved me, of course!"

- "I didn't spend much time with my co-workers. I like to focus on the task at hand. Still, I got along with everyone in the office."

_____

_____

_____

_____

_____

What did you think of your boss?

- "I respected the fact that my boss had a harder job than I."

- "Well, we didn't always see eye-to-eye but we worked well together."

- NEVER speak poorly of a previous employer.

_____
_____
_____
_____
_____

How did you do in school?

- "I was an average student. I'm glad this isn't school. I much prefer this type of work."

- Obviously, if you did well in school, say so. Most of us, however, were indeed average. Just remember to point out that you will do better for an employer than you did for your teachers.

_____
_____
_____
_____
_____

What were your favorite and least favorite subjects?

- This is another question to see if you are well-suited to the job. If you were active in the drama program and are applying for a position as a bookkeeper, it may not be a good match.

_____
_____
_____
_____
_____

What kind of hours are you used to working?

- "I am used to doing whatever is required of me."

- "I am used to a day job, though I am happy to put in any overtime that's needed."

- "I am under the impression that this position is from 8-5. Those hours work well for me."

- If the employer asks this question, there is a good chance that overtime is involved with the position, or odd hours. Either way, if you are not interested in overtime because you have children, perhaps, or do not want to work a graveyard shift, now is the time to find out. If you are able to work any shift and any number of hours, then the first answer is definitely a good one.

_____

_____

_____

_____

_____

What salary do you require?

- Turn this back into a question. "How much are you expecting to pay?" Or, "What is the salary range for someone with my skills and experience?"

- "In your newspaper ad, it says that the position pay $8-10 per hour. I'm certainly happy to start in that range."

- The employer wants to find out if you want less money than they are planning to pay (which makes you appear less valuable and less skilled) or more money than they are planning to pay (in which case, you will cost too much for their budget). Asking a question will allow you to find out what they have in mind (and most employers do have a salary figure in mind).

- The second answer lets the employer know that you're aware of their pay rate and willing to work at that level.

_____

_____

_____

_____

_____

Are you willing to be drug tested?

• "Yes, I am. I'll do whatever it takes to get this job."

• Drugs have been known to decrease both an employee's awareness of safety issues and their productivity. Employers today want drug-free employees and almost all employers are testing to make sure that new hires are drug-free. Some employers even continue with random testing throughout the period of employment. Most drug tests can detect anything that has been in your system within the last thirty days. However, some employers use hair-testing, which will find drugs in your system from the past six months.

_____

_____

_____

_____

_____

Have you ever had your driver's license revoked?

• "No."

• "Will driving be a part of my work here?"

• "No" is the best answer. However, if you have had your driver's license revoked, you do not want to lie in the interview. Remember, some employers will review your state records and this is a matter of public record. If this is a driving-related job, this question does have some relevance to the position. But, if you have had your license revoked, it should not be necessary to tell the employer for most jobs as most jobs do not actually require driving.

_____

_____

_____

_____

_____

How/Why would you be an asset to our company?

- "Because you want someone who will do a good job and be happy about it. I'm that person."

- Again, this answer should apply to the position and let the employer know that you are the right person for the job.

_____

_____

_____

_____

_____

Can we call your previous/current employer?

- "Yes. The phone number is (888) 888-8888."

- "I would rather you didn't. If you'd like to know about my work habits, you can call my previous employer at (123) 456-7899."

- The interviewer probably wants to hear, from your current employer, that you are a good worker. However, if your current employer doesn't know that you're looking for a new job, then use one of your other references.

_____

_____

_____

_____

_____

Can you give us references/recommendations?

- "Certainly, here is a list of my references."

- "Gladly. You can call my teacher at (998) 765-4321 and my accountant at (887) 654-4321."

- Most employers will want to talk to someone to find out whether or not you are as good as you say you are. Be prepared with names and phone numbers of your former employers, and responsibly-employed friends, as well as counselors and teachers.

_____
_____
_____
_____
_____

Are you willing to travel or relocate?

- "Yes, I'm happy to go wherever you want me to."

- "Yes, I'm more than willing to travel in this area."

- "No. I was under the impression that this job was stationary. That's why I am applying for it."

- If you are willing and able to travel or relocate, let the employer know. If not, say so, but in a positive way.

_____
_____
_____
_____
_____

What are your short-/long-term goals?

- "Honestly, my immediate goal is to get this job."

- "I have one primary goal right now, to get this job. Once I'm employed, I'll review my long-term goals." Or, "Once I find a better position than the one I'm in now, I'll review my long-term goals."

- "Short-term? I would like to get this job. In the long term, I am looking forward to a career in this field, a new car, and, eventually, a nice house."

- Many people haven't thought about their long-term goals. If you're keeping up with the day-to-day details of paying bills, keeping house and raising children, then that is understandable. Still, the employer should know that you want this job *and* that you see future benefits to working. Now is the perfect time to tell him or her. Also, the most successful individuals in this world know what they want, short-term and long-term (though they don't always say it).

Are you looking for permanent or temporary work?

- Answer this question according to the type of job you are applying for: permanent, temporary, or temp-to-perm.

- Remember, there are advantages and disadvantages with each type of situation.

Tell me something about yourself.

- Remember, the employer should only be concerned with work-related details. So, this question should really be, "Tell me about yourself as regards this job." *Do not* tell the employer details about your personal life: age, marital status, children, substance or domestic abuse issues, etc. Tell the employer the top three to five reasons why s/he should hire you. "I am strong, capable, dependable, experienced, responsible." "I have a variety of experience, as well as good people skills and good computer skills."

_____

_____

What are your strengths?

• Strengths may include: resourceful, team-oriented, dependable, always on time, get along well with others, independent, able to follow directions, good problem-solving skills, good listening skills, good computer skills, detail-oriented, etc. Choose your top three strengths and tell the interviewer.

_____

_____

_____

_____

_____

What are your weaknesses?

• You may want to use some humor here. For example, "Ice cream." Or, "Chocolate."

• You might answer this question is by using a weakness that can also be seen as a strength. There are three basic weakness/strength combinations. (1) "I am a workaholic. I guess it's bad in that I often work too hard and don't get the rest that I should. Of course, you can be sure that I am always working hard for you." (2) "I am a bit of a perfectionist. So, I take a little longer to get the job done, but it is always done right." (3) "I am very detail-oriented. So, I take a little longer to get the job done, but the details are always in place." *It's important* that you choose a weakness/strength combination that is accurate for you, because the employer may expect you to work accordingly. In other words, if you say that you are a workaholic, the employer may expect you to give plenty of overtime.

• You might come clean about something relatively small. For example, "It sometimes takes me awhile to remember names, but I've gotten better at this over the years."

_____

_____

_____

_____

_____

How do you feel about working for an older/younger supervisor?

- "I'm flexible."

- "I can work for any boss you give me. After all, they're the boss."

- If you feel resentful of your boss simply because they are older or younger than you, it will cause a strain in your work attitude right away. An employer would rather hire someone who can give every boss a chance to prove that s/he is a good boss (whether or not it's true).

_____

_____

_____

_____

_____

What can I do for you?

- "Hire me."

- "Give me this job."

_____

_____

_____

_____

_____

What kind of people irritate you?

- "No one, really, except people who get in the way of my work."

- It is best to indicate that you are easy to get along with, but that you are focused on your work and do not like those who cause disruptions.

_____
_____
_____
_____
_____

Don't you think you are over-qualified for this job?

- This is a polite way of saying that you used to earn more money than they are willing to pay you now. You should focus your answer on the skill-based orientation of the question. For example, "While I am highly qualified for certain aspects of this position, I also see a number of ways that I could learn and grow in this job."

_____
_____
_____
_____
_____

Don't you think you are under-qualified for this job?

- This question indicates that you used to earn less money than the salary they expected for this position, and if you didn't earn that amount, perhaps you are not worth the money. It is a question that is designed to put you on the defensive. Show your strengths. "I may be a weak typist, but my telephone skills are exceptional."

_____
_____
_____
_____
_____

What motivates you?

- If a person isn't motivated, they may have attitude problems or an inability to really last in the job. Remember to avoid bringing your personal life into an interview. While your children may motivate you, speak of your desire to create a healthy and happy future for yourself.

_____

_____

_____

_____

_____

How do you work under pressure?

- "I am deadline-oriented and respond well to pressure."

- "I prefer a position with a balanced, steady flow of work; though, I understand that all jobs have their busy seasons and I am always prepared for those."

_____

_____

_____

_____

_____

How do you work on your own?

- "Great! It gives me a chance to focus on the task at hand."

- "I prefer being given strong direction and guidelines. With that, I can do the job either on my own or with a team."

_____

_____

_____

_____

_____

Give an example of: your creativity, your analytical skills, your administrative skills, your leadership skills. Or, "What would you do if…"

- Some employers will ask these sorts of questions, usually for higher-level positions. Often, the challenge here is to give a work-related example instead of a personal example. Give some thought now to your work, school and travel-related experiences that may prove valuable in future jobs and interviews. Use them as examples.

_____

_____

_____

_____

_____

Do you consider yourself a competitive person? Why or why not?

- "I am always competing with myself, to improve my own skills."

- "No, I prefer a team-oriented atmosphere."

_____

_____

_____

_____

_____

Have you done any volunteer work?

- "You bet I have! I believe in giving to the community and I've volunteered at the YWCA for several years."

- Remember, successful people share their success. Every non-profit agency where you may have been a client in the past also depends on professional volunteers. Some of those agencies may have required 'volunteer' work in order for you to receive their benefits. Also, work required by General Relief or welfare programs, as well as Community Service, counts as volunteer work in most instances.

_____
_____
_____
_____
_____

Why do you think you'd like this job?

• Well, why do you think you would like the job? Is it close to home and easy to get to? Is it in line with your skills? Is it just the job for someone like yourself? Whatever you do, don't say, "Because of the money." Money is a given, employers want to hire those who have higher values.

_____
_____
_____
_____
_____

How do you respond to instruction/criticism?

• "I always figure that the boss knows something that I don't, so I will listen to whatever the boss says. Of course, I respond best when it's coupled with positive comments, too."

_____
_____
_____
_____
_____

What types of books have you read recently?

• "To be honest, I've been reading the classifieds and looking for work, and I haven't had time for any extra reading."

- "The last book I read was Dale Carnegie's <u>How to Win Friends and Influence People</u>, since then I've been focused on finding a new job."

- If you have been reading a good book, tell the interviewer. However, do not mention that you've been reading this book or any book that could be considered controversial. By all means, do not tell the interviewer that you have read something that you haven't read. If they've read it, and want to talk about it, you will be embarrassed.

_____
_____
_____
_____
_____

<u>What do you look for in a supervisor?</u>

- "I can work very well on my own, but I like a boss who communicates well."

- "I like a boss who is firm but supportive."

- "A boss is responsible for the functioning of the office. I like a boss who sets priorities and supports their completion."

- The interviewer is trying to determine if you will work well with your potential supervisor. Your answer should be general so that you do not offend the person interviewing you and aren't disqualified because they're worried that you won't get along with the boss. On the other hand, if you want to know more about your potential supervisor, ask. If he is the type that is always looking over your shoulder, now is the time to find out!

_____
_____
_____
_____
_____

Some Questions Do Not Pertain To Your Ability To Do The Job

These questions are illegal and should not be asked in an interview. However, they *are* still asked in interviews. Some employers simply do not know the laws. Other employers want to see what they can get away with and this is their way of getting information that they want.

Either answer these questions honestly (without going into detail) OR answer these questions by saying "I don't see how that applies to my ability to do the job." Emphasize that this job is your first priority. Remember, you can't afford your other priorities unless you have a job!

How many children do you have at home?
What are the ages of your children?
Who will babysit your children?
Do you plan to have any more children?
Are you currently practicing birth control?
What are your plans for marriage?
Are you currently living with your husband?
How long have you been married/divorced/separated?
Do you still see your ex-husband?
Is your present husband the father of your children?
Is your family dependent on your paycheck?
How does your family feel about you working?
Are your parents U.S. citizens?
Where are your parents living?
How long have you been a U.S. citizen?
What is your native tongue/language?
What kind of a name is that?
Were you born in this country?
When did you come to the U.S.?
What is your mother's maiden name?
Were you in the military?
Why were you not in the military?
What clubs/organizations do you belong to?
Are you active in any political organizations/campaigns/parties?
How do you spend your weekends/evenings?

Where do you go to church?
What is your religious preference?
Have you ever been arrested?
Have you ever had trouble with the law?
Have you ever been subpoenaed?
Have you ever had any property repossessed/foreclosed?
Do you own your own home?
Are you renting or buying your home?
Do you live in a house or an apartment?
Do you own your own car?
How did you finance your education?

Note: The only legal question regarding 'trouble with the law' is, "Have you been convicted of a crime?"

Questions For You To Ask

At the beginning or end of most interviews, you will be asked if you have any questions. It is best for you if this is asked at the beginning of the interview because then you will be able to target your answers depending on what you already know. Any way that you look at it, these questions are suitable for you to ask in almost any interview. And, yes, it makes you look good if you have questions to ask. It shows that you're interested in the job and want to know more about it. Similar questions are grouped together so that you can avoid repeating yourself.

- Why is this position open?

- What have been the primary reasons for employees leaving in the past?

- Why did the last person leave?

- Could you describe the job responsibilities in more detail?

- What would you like done differently by the next person who fills this position?

- What are some of the goals that you would like accomplished?

- What are the longer-term objectives?

- How much autonomy/freedom would I have in performing these duties?

- What support would I receive toward accomplishing these goals?

- What are some of the difficulties of this position? How do you think these would best be handled?

- What is the natural upward progression from this position? What is the time frame for promotions?

- Does this company usually promote from within?

- What sort of training is available for those who wish to advance in this company?

- In your opinion, in what ways has this organization been most successful recently?

- What significant changes do you foresee?

- How are employees evaluated? How is success measured?

- How did you get your position?

- When do you expect to make a decision regarding this position?

- When can I start?

Upon Leaving

- DO wait until the interviewer ends the interview.

- DO make sure to ask the interviewer for his/her business card.

- DO shake hands firmly.

- DO say "THANK YOU" to your interviewer(s). Use their names.

- DON'T run out of the interview early.

- DON'T walk out without saying thank you.

By waiting for the interviewer to end the interview, you are showing patience and respect. Also, you are making sure that s/he gets all the information that s/he wants.

Post Interview

- <u>DO</u> send a thank you note to all who interviewed you. This point cannot be overemphasized. If you are the only applicant to send a thank you note, it will put you head-and-shoulders above the rest. Doing this will show the employer that you (a) are serious about wanting the position and (b) pay attention to follow-up.

- DO send thank you letters after second and third interviews as well.

- DO consider sending a thank you to the secretary also.

Thank you notes do not need to be long or typewritten. If you want, use a note-card and write your note. There is a sample thank you message on page 96.

Now What Happens?

If the employer still likes you at this point, he or she will check your references as listed on the application. They may also run a credit check regarding your financial position or a criminal records check. The legality and accuracy of these checks may be questionable; however, they are relatively easy to complete and becoming more common all the time.

Don't worry! If the employer truly likes you, they will often give you a chance to explain any problems in your past. During the second interview (or on the telephone before the second interview), the employer will ask about anything that concerns him from these background checks. If the employer comes back to you and says something to the effect of, "Your most recent employer didn't speak very highly of you…," you should respond by reminding them of your comments in the interview. For example, "As I said in the interview, my employer and I had a different opinion about the work I should be doing. I'm sure that influenced his/

her opinion of my overall performance. I do feel confident that I'm clear on the duties involved in this position and I'm committed to this company as a whole, no matter how my job description may change over time." Remember, by indicating a differing opinion than that of your former employer, your potential employer may be concerned that you won't perform on this job simply because you don't agree with your job description. It is important that you indicate your commitment to the job. They aren't likely to hire you just to "stand there and look good."

If, when they ran a criminal records check on you, they found something from your past, you want to be able to respond with, "Had you asked, I would have gladly told you during our interview. That offense was definitely in my past and I'd like to leave it there. Now, I'm looking to continue my future in a more positive direction with this job."

FOLLOW-UP

Why Follow-up?

1. Because the employer is busy and will forget you.

2. Because the employer is interested in a quality staff person who is committed to details and follow-through which you show when you follow through on the interview.

3. Because the employer is interested in those applicants who are interested in their company and follow-up is a way of showing your interest.

Jim Stoneface, who runs the sales office at a major hotel, considers follow-up so important that it's a piece of the interview. He was asked once to interview a friend of a friend, which he did, because she needed a second chance. He was both surprised and happy with her honesty and integrity on the application which listed her prison work experience. At the end of the interview, he told her that he liked her and would like to talk to her again, after he had a chance to review the upcoming work schedules. Finally, he asked her to call him back on Monday.

She never called. But, if she had, he would have hired her.

Remember, the employer has *one* job and *many* people who want that job. It's reasonable for the employer to use a variety of tests in order to determine who will best do the job.

How to Follow-up

1. At the end of the interview: Leave your list of references. Ask for a business card. Ask the question, "When do you expect to make a decision regarding this position?" This will determine how quickly you must act. You should act within 24 hours.

2. Write a thank-you note: A thank you note will remind the employer who you are and what your strengths are a few days after the interview. It should be short, sweet and to the point. It may be handwritten, if your writing is good, or typed.

Dear Ms. Barbie,

Thank you for taking the time yesterday to interview me for the Basket weaving position. I'd like to reiterate my interest in working at Barbie's Basket weavers.

My skills in weaving and dedication to quality work will certainly enhance your current situation.

Please feel free to call me at 999-999-9999 with any further questions you may have. I look forward to hearing from you.

Sincerely, J.J. Hardworker
999-999-9999

---

3. Call: about 3 days after you mail the letter or on the day they plan to make their decision. Ask for the person that you interviewed with. A sample conversation may go something like this: "Hello, this is J.J. Hardworker. I'm just calling to check on the status of the 'Blah-Blah' position." They should have a response for you. Either,

- they were waiting for the first person who bothered to call and check on the position, and you're hired;

- they've made the decision and you're not qualified;

- they're interested in you for a different position and would like a second interview; or

- they're really swamped and haven't made a decision yet. If they haven't made the decision yet, ask when you should call back. Generally, every Wednesday is a safe bet.

If they want a second interview, it's a good thing. They wouldn't waste time or money interviewing you, if you weren't under serious consideration.

6

Show What You Know

JOB OFFER!

HOW TO GET AHEAD

Now that you've been hired, and not before, you will have a chance to show this employer how good you are at doing what needs to be done. Because you were applying for jobs that were appropriate for your skills and interests, this should be easy. While some employers now use pre-employment tests, many employers do not—which means that this is your first chance to prove yourself.

This is actually some of the most important information in this book because it will help you be successful in this job which will make you more successful in the working world.

Getting this job was just the first step of many in turning your life around. Very few entry-level jobs pay well these days. Eventually, you'll probably seek a raise, a promotion or a new job at a new company. For now, though, excelling at this job will establish you as a responsible member of the "working world." *It is best to keep this job for at least one year.* One year is seen as a benchmark of stability, dependability and commitment by many employers.

There was a time when the information on the following pages would move you forward. Nowadays, they will merely help you keep the job. Remember, your work is always being compared to the work of your co-workers. Also, remember that the business owner is in business to make money. If s/he makes money, then s/he can afford to pay you and the rest of the staff. If s/he does not make money, s/he will have to lay someone off.

There is something else that you should know about employment. While the employer may only be paying you minimum wage, s/he is also paying Social Security taxes, Unemployment taxes, and Worker's Compensation insurance for you, as well as any health benefits you may receive. That means that you may actually cost up to $10.00 per hour (even though you're earning only minimum wage)! You're not free to the employer and it is your job to be worth more than your paycheck because you're costing more than your paycheck.

The good news is this: according to a study in the Orange County Register, you have three months in which to prove yourself and show that you are worth it. So, don't worry. Three months is plenty of time in which to make a good impression. They won't expect a new hire to be brilliant right away.

On the following two pages are a few simple "rules" that will make this job work for you.

- Arrive clean and neat and appropriately dressed. Remember that the employer depends on customers for business. The customer prefers a clean staff person. Also, your co-workers prefer a clean co-worker.

- You get to work on time or a few minutes earlier.

- You stay at work until your shift is over or fifteen to thirty minutes later.

- You work through some of your breaks and maybe even through your lunch.

- You do your work. Don't spend time on the phone with children, family or friends unless absolutely necessary. Remember, this job earns you the money to spend on rent, food, clothing, health care, trips to the amusement park, whatever. But, the employer is paying you to work. On the plus side, this paycheck is probably larger than a welfare check. Your costs may be higher now, too, especially if you have to pay for childcare. Fortunately, employers typically give raises more often than welfare and other government programs.

- When you run out of work, ask if there is anything else you can do.

- Ask questions if you are unsure. It's better to do it right the first time than to have to correct your mistakes. Take notes so that you don't have to repeat the same questions. They know you're new and realize that you have things to learn. Asking questions shows them that you're interested in doing your job correctly.

- Ask if there is anything else you can do.

- Act friendly but NOT gossip-y. One easy mistake that my clients make is talking about their pasts with fellow employees during their first few months on the job. "Wow, man, it's hard to believe I was in the pen just a few short months ago..." will not impress your co-workers and may encourage them to find reasons you shouldn't have the job. Remember, your past is your past. If you want to talk about something, then talk about your future. "I'm really looking forward to the day when I can buy a new car."

- Don't take sides in any situation. Have you heard of office politics? EVERY office has them. When you are new, you don't know who has the real power so it's best to remain neutral. Otherwise, you may find yourself out of a job with your "friend."

- Stay healthy and make sure your kids stay healthy. As a matter of fact, during the first 90 days, if you get sick, you should go in to work anyway! If you're really sick, they'll send you home. Plus, they'll know that you're serious about this job!

- Keep notes on your successes (i.e. what you've learned, compliments from fellow staff and/or customers, improvements you've made, etc.). Keep these on hand for your performance evaluation. They show your value.

- When you bring a problem to the boss, also bring possible solutions. Watch your attitude and tone of voice. Nobody likes a whiner!

- Don't ask for days off unless absolutely necessary! Give as much notice as possible when you need time off. You were hired because the employer needs someone to do work. If you're not at the office, they still need the work to get done.

Shamus Frank, an ex-felon, got a job in a warehouse and was doing well initially, according to the employer. However, he lost his job when he missed three days of work during his 90-day probationary period. You be the judge...

Day 1: Missed because his car was impounded. The employment-viewpoint: Take a bus or call a friend with a car! Call and let the employer know that you will be late, but still go to work. After all, won't you need your paycheck to pay to get your car out of storage?

Day 2: Missed because of a niece's funeral. The employment-viewpoint: Probably had enough advance warning that the employer should have known ahead of time. He could've taken a half-day and worked the rest of the day. Besides, this was an ex-felon, had he still been in prison, he wouldn't even have had a choice...

Day 3: It doesn't matter anymore because this is the day that he lost the job.

If you were the boss, would you have given him another chance?

There are <u>NO ifs, ands or buts</u> about these rules! There are far too many other people who would like your job. Besides, if you want to turn your life around, you want this job to last at least one year. It's probably time for you to establish some stability. Then you can move forward with your life.

You can change your clothes, your mind, your attitude right now! You can change your life! The world is full of success stories if you look for them.

About the Author

Camille Leon

Camille Leon, the author, has managed several Employment Services agencies and programs for disadvantaged youth and adults. She has worked with clients both individually and in groups, providing training and advice to thousands of job-seekers. She has taught job-seekers in employment workshops, as well as volunteers and staff members in 'Train the Trainer' sessions.

Leon continues to speak to disadvantaged job-seekers on a regular basis. She is a public speaker and coach working with individuals in all areas of the socio-economic spectrum to improve their quality of living and working. She believes that image and integrity will increase your impact...and your income!

For more information about booking Camille for a speaking or training engagement, please contact her at:

P.O. Box 66880, Los Angeles, CA, 90066
310-398-4214 or (fax) 928-447-3454
WAVEgeneration@hotmail.com

0-595-27116-2